I0819203

THE LORAfied
COOKBOOK

Easy Recipes and
Budget-Friendly Hacks
to Feed the Whole Family

Lora McLaughlin Peterson

with Susan Puckett

Publisher Mike Sanders
Art & Design Director William Thomas
Editorial Director Ann Barton
Executive Editor Olivia Peluso
Senior Designer Jessica Lee
Designer Robert Byron Jones
Editorial Assistant Resham Anand
Photographer Ivan Solis
Food Stylist Marian Cairns
Prop Stylist Amy Paliwoda
Recipe Tester Bee Berrie
Copyeditor Mira S. Park
Proofreaders West Matuszak & Bianca Bosman
Indexer Beverlee Day

First American Edition, 2026
Published in the United States by DK Publishing
1745 Broadway, 20th Floor, New York, NY 10019

The authorized representative in the EEA is Dorling Kindersley Verlag GmbH. Arnulfstr. 124, 80636 Munich, Germany

25 26 27 28 29 10 9 8 7 6 5 4 3 2 1
001–348307–May/2026

A catalog record for this book
is available from the Library of Congress.
ISBN 978-0-5939-6503-0

DK books are available at special discounts when purchased in bulk for sales promotions, premiums, fund-raising, or educational use. For details, contact SpecialSales@dk.com

Printed and bound in China

www.dk.com

This book was made with Forest Stewardship Council™ certified paper – one small step in DK's commitment to a sustainable future.
Learn more at
www.dk.com/uk/information/sustainability

To my amazing mom, Norma Jean, the original Life Hacker. You're a true inspiration. I won the mother lottery with you!

To my dearest Scooter, Betsy, Emmy, and Jack, my first four followers, for being my cheerleaders when the bleachers were still empty. Thank you for always letting me be me, no matter how embarrassing. I love you more than anything and always will!

And to the memory of my dad, Harold. I lost you too young, but boy, when you were here, it sure was great! I drew so much inspiration from you. I hope I've made you proud.

Contents

Introduction

Welcome to my crazy life, where spinning plates and keeping kids, dogs, and Trader Joe's herb plants alive are my specialty. Oh, and a husband . . . guess I kind of count him as one of the kids, LOL! Whether you already know me through social media or you didn't even know I existed until you picked up this book, I'm thrilled you're here!

If you're looking for recipes that don't cost a fortune to make and don't take a lot of time, then you've come to the right place. If the only way you can get your family's attention each night is by screaming (or texting) "Dinner is ready!" I've got you covered. And if you're craving something comforting and homemade you can easily make tonight that leaves you with enough bandwidth to watch that Netflix show you're into, then this is for you!

I'm Lora McLaughlin Peterson, the creator of LORAfied, a digital media company I started in 2021 to help people do life better on a budget. It's always so gratifying to hear from my followers—now more than two million and counting!—how much they appreciate that my recipes are as quick and easy as they sound, and most don't require even an ounce of patience. I'm tickled pink when they tell me how my simple hack for removing potato peels—instantly, without a peeler—has been life-changing . . . not to mention so easy even the kids could do it!

I am not a trained chef, and I'm not out to set the culinary world on fire with cutting-edge innovations. My cooking style is rooted in my small-town upbringing in Kansas, where sloppy joes and Salisbury steak never fell out of fashion and the words "amuse-bouche" and "sommelier" are only heard on the Food Network. The home-cooked meals I was raised on were simple and delicious. Unassuming, but not boring. Well-seasoned, but not crazy—meaning you can recognize what you're eating. You leave the table full but not stuffed.

That's still the kind of food that gets my picky-eating family excited to come to the table today at our home in Los Angeles, whether a recipe is straight from the splattered page of an old family cookbook, or a new creation inspired by a favorite menu item, or a curiosity that's gone viral on the internet. I believe that the positive energy that comes from sitting at a table with people you love is underrated these days, and I'm trying to bring it back.

How I Became "That Helpful Mom"

So how did I come to this mid-life career path? Why is thriftiness ingrained in me? And why am I on a mission to help bring families back together at the dinner table?

It's something I've thought about for years, starting when I became a divorced single mom at the age of 26. Struggling to pay the rent in LA and hell-bent on not going into debt, I sold my wedding ring to pay my divorce attorney bills. I shut off my cell phone and cancelled everything that wasn't necessary.

I'll never forget that Monday when, after I'd paid all of my bills, I was horrified to discover I had only $15 left in my bank account. I hadn't been to the grocery store and wasn't going to get paid again until Friday. At that moment, I knew something had to change.

I had two choices: (A) Take my baby girl and go running back to my supportive family in Kansas, or (B) figure out how to stretch my meager salary to get by as a rookie TV reporter in one of the world's most expensive cities. The first option was too depressing to contemplate. I'd dreamed of becoming a TV reporter since I was a child, watching the nightly news with my dad, and even started a school newspaper in the fourth grade. And now here I was, reporting on TV in Los Angeles! I'd come too far to turn back now.

So I went with plan B. I cut out most restaurant meals, clipped coupons, and figured out when and where to find the best bargains. I never bought more than I knew I could use—ever! I became adept at stretching two bananas over a week's worth of cereal and making a tasty chicken salad with the remnants of a roast chicken and a chopped apple that I could grab from the fridge when I got home late from work.

No matter how long my work hours or how tight my budget, I made sure my daughter and I had wholesome balanced meals together, the way my family did back in Kansas.

As the youngest of nine kids (yes, I was an "oops baby"!), I grew up surrounded by enthusiastic cooks who instilled that value in me. My dad owned a chain of restaurants specializing in burgers called The White Grill, modeled after the White Castle where he'd worked as a teenager. President Harry S. Truman was actually a fan of my dad's burgers, calling them the "best damn hamburgers I ever ate."

All but one had a full-service dining room that served a full menu of Kansas/Southern comfort food—well, our version of it. Fried chicken dinners were a signature. Folks would line up for them, especially on Sundays after church. All of my older siblings helped in the restaurants, but as the spoiled-rotten baby of the family, I was too young. My spot was on the beanbag in the office.

At home, my mom, Norma Jean (who's 95 as of this writing and still going strong!), was—and still is—the best comfort food cook in the world. Even though she was an incredibly accomplished businesswoman, she saw to it that we sat down together at the table every night, with cloth napkins and real plates—never paper or plastic. Chicken-fried steak, biscuits and gravy, Sunday pot roast, fried chicken, fried fish, homemade French fries—you name it, she cooked it. There's just no way to explain the magic my mom can perform with salt, pepper, butter, and maybe a little garlic powder. My husband, Scooter, and I joke that she and Bobby Flay both have that "umami" gene!

I carried those lessons with me when I left home to get a journalism degree from California State University. Those Midwestern values kept me grounded as I made a new home in Los Angeles, swapped out my biscuits-and-gravy breakfasts for detox smoothies, and got comfortable in front of TV cameras reporting the day's news. I covered it all, from brush fires to crime scenes to the Oscars.

Eventually I made the jump to network news and moved up to bigger assignments—and paychecks. During those years, I landed many incredible interviews, including with Hillary Clinton and Oprah Winfrey, and covered some of the nation's biggest news stories. I was grateful my career also allowed me to work some lighthearted, uplifting pieces into my schedule, especially those aimed at the multitude of women I could easily relate to who were also striving to do life better for themselves and their families on a budget but with a little flair. In the early 2000s, I hosted a popular segment called "All About You," where I showed viewers how to live a fabulous lifestyle for less, earning me the title of "The Budget Martha Stewart."

Meanwhile, I dated a lot, got engaged and basically left at the altar, and then met a handsome businessman I was seated next to on a puddle jumper en route to the courthouse to cover the Scott Peterson murder trial. Imagine my surprise to learn his name was Scott Peterson as well! But fortunately, to avoid confusion, everyone calls him Scooter. To say we hit it off is an understatement. We got married, added two more kids (Kid 2 and Kid 3 in these pages) to the family, and our romance continues at home in Los Angeles on the exact site where *Dukes of Hazzard* was shot. I continued to freelance for various media companies until I finally decided I'd had enough of the erratic schedules and left to focus on raising my family and doing charity work, thinking that would be enough for me. I was wrong.

Although I enjoyed having more time to cook, do creative things around the house, and tag along with Scooter, often with kids in tow, on business trips and vacations, I wasn't helping anyone outside my own little world. I found myself growing restless to do something more.

In January of 2021, while the world was still reeling from a global pandemic, Kid 1—by then a 29-year-old independent career woman—and her best friend (I call her Kid 1.5) showed me the way. They suggested I make online videos where I could dispense tips and hacks on everything from cooking to basic housekeeping, as I'd done for them after they'd gone off to college. I was used to them calling or texting me regularly for an easy recipe that would save them from another fast-food night or for tips on how to do a basic chore like folding a fitted sheet.

"LORAfied" was the word the girls used when I would show them how to turn something simple into something they thought was "magical." The first time they used it, we were decorating gingerbread houses together. Everyone else was done within thirty minutes, while I kept going for four hours straight and ended up making an edible Barbie Dreamhouse. The girls did a slideshow of their creations on Instagram and included a photo of mine with a caption that read, "This one has been LORAfied."

And that's how LORAfied started.

From that point on, my millennial "advisors" told me that I needed to figure out how to start posting my own Instagram recipes and videos. A few months later, they insisted that I get on TikTok as well. And let me tell you, the learning curve was steep! I'd had experience being in front of the camera with a microphone at fires and crime scenes and on the red carpet interviewing A-list celebrities at the Oscars. I even had a bit part playing myself in the movie *Four Christmases*, starring Reese Witherspoon and Vince Vaughn. But I had never had to edit or shoot anything in my entire news career.

My first attempts were unintentionally pretty hilarious. I spewed coffee all over my kitchen counter when I tried to demonstrate how I made my high-protein, zero-carb mocha coffee with an electric milk frother. My husband and kids sometimes popped up in the background, having just rolled out of bed, as unsuspecting extras in my fledgling mini-productions. Yet my audience didn't seem to mind my mishaps; instead, they cheered me on in the comments. I quickly came to love directly connecting with people wherever they were in their lives, sharing practical, sometimes a little whimsical, and often delicious things to boost their day.

Now it's part of my daily routine to check in with my online followers right after I take my gremlin fur babies, Tippy and Tiger, for their morning walk. I'll invite them to follow me at various points throughout the day, whether I'm scouting for savings on name-brand body wash dupes at Dollar Tree, spraying overripe fruit with silver and gold paint for a no-cost holiday tablescape, or packing fifteen days of clothes in one suitcase for an overseas trip.

Then for my final check-in, "it's time to talk dinner!," where I show exactly what we're eating that night. I may show how I roast a complete chicken dinner in an upside-down Bundt pan. Or if I'm too tired to cook, I might just toss a simple salad to go with the takeout pizza Scooter brought in. I'll film as we all begin to serve ourselves—no stopping for garnishing or food styling. What you see is what we eat. My hope is to take away all of the "things" we think we need to do to have a proper meal and focus on what's important: sharing that meal with those you love. Or if you're alone, just taking a minute to put your food on a real plate and taking a seat with a cloth napkin can be a game changer.

I want people to know they can come to the table as they are, with a meal they have assembled with love, and their dinner will be a success. The old line "good enough is better than perfect" should be painted on the walls of every kitchen!

Read on and let me show you how feeding yourself and your family well, no matter how little time you have or how tight your budget, is easier than you think. And trust me: The payoff will be huge.

2 pc. 1.10
3 pc.
4 pc.
WHITE Grill
Hwy. 54 and 69
CLOSE COVER FOR SAFETY
SERVED AFTER 11:00 A.M. ON SUNDAYS
SERVED IN DINING ROOM ON SUNDAYS
Sandwiches
Jumbo Cheeseburger with Tomato
Cheeseburger
Hamburger
Ham and Egg
Ham on Bun
Ham with Barbeque Sauce
Bacon and Tomato
Ham and Cheese, grilled
Cheese, grilled
French Fries
Baked Potato with Butter
(Sour Cream .45)
Chili (we make our own)
Pie (we make our own)
With Ice Cream
Soup—tomato, chicken noodle, split pea, bean, vegetable
Old Fashioned Bean Soup
Drinks
Sanka Coffee .15
Buttermilk
Tea
Dr. Pepper, 7-Up, RC, Pepsi, Root Beer
Chocolate or Cherry
History
Waffles
CURB SERVICE
4 HAMBURGERS TO GO $1.

Lora
FIED

The LORAfied Promises

The promises I make to my readers throughout the book tie back to these core philosophies:

1. Home cooking doesn't have to be a chore. The key is having a positive mindset and a few tricks up your sleeve. Instead of buying expensive, prepackaged, or home-delivered meals, I will show you how you can make something just as satisfying with one pan and three ingredients. Get out your white plates and grab some colorful cloth napkins—I promise your chicken will taste better!

2. "100 percent made from scratch" is overrated. Meals that are "half-homemade" still deserve 100 percent credit if they get the family to the table for a balanced meal. There's no shame in using a taco seasoning blend or a high-quality bottled spaghetti sauce to simplify the cooking process and save you from buying ingredients you'll never use up—it's smart. And never underestimate the allure of the canned crescent roll or reimagined cake mix, shortcuts that deliver *big*! I do read labels and cruise the produce aisles for wholesome ingredients, but I also believe no one should feel shame in taking the easy way out with instant pudding mix, dough from a cardboard tube, frozen meatballs, or a bottle of ranch dressing now and then.

3. The right kitchen tools can make mealtimes infinitely more enjoyable and relaxing if you know what's out there. I don't advocate for acquiring more gadgets and appliances than you'll use—especially when space is an issue. Instead, assess your needs and habits carefully and stock your kitchen accordingly. I will call attention to the everyday tools and newfangled gizmos that have made my life in the kitchen easier and more fun.

4. You can stick to a healthy eating regimen while allowing for "cheats" and without putting the whole family on a diet. I'm neither a doctor nor a nutritionist, so I would never dispense health advice. But because so many of my followers ask me how I stay fit, despite having an insatiable sweet tooth, I will share what works for me. I am a poster child for osteoporosis, so reducing sugar and carbs and making sure I get enough protein has made a massive difference for me. But the idea of constantly being "on a diet" sounds dreadful. I had to come up with a way to give myself permission to have the things I love, without wrecking my health or forcing everyone else at my table to sacrifice. Cheat days are a must! No guilt, just enjoy. The old saying "you can't exercise your way out of a bad diet" is real, but one treat now and then isn't a diet—it's just a well-deserved break.

I abide roughly by the 90/10 diet plan of striving to eat healthy 90 percent of the time, while giving myself permission to eat whatever I want 10 percent of the time. I have found that having indulgences to look forward to, rather than swearing off any one food completely, gives me the psychological comfort I need to keep from falling off the wagon and enjoy regular meals with my family without feeling deprived.

5. You can feed yourself and your family delicious, nutritious, high-quality meals without paying top dollar at the grocery store. Those lean years of struggling to pay bills taught me lessons in smart shopping, bargain-hunting, and creatively using up leftovers that I carry with me to this day. I still strive to never pay full price for anything I don't have to!

6. You'll learn the mental value of maintaining a tidy kitchen. I'll never go full Marie Kondo on you, although I think she's pretty talented. But I do offer some simple tips and hacks for minimizing dirty dishes and cluttered countertops. If you do nothing else today, make your bed in the morning and do the dishes before you go to bed at night. I promise, your home will instantly look better. You'll be surprised at the positive emotional value it adds as well.

Now let's head on into the kitchen and get started!

Welcome to My Curated Kitchen

A Neatnik's Guide to Making Your Kitchen Your Sanctuary

Like many moms and people who work from home, I spend a good portion of the day and night in my kitchen. I believe it should be a place where I can de-stress rather than stir up anxiety, and I've spent a lifetime creating rituals for doing just that. I run the dishwasher every night, no matter how much or little is in there. It's nice to start the day with clean dishes and an empty dishwasher even if it only lasts a few minutes around here. Same with countertops: wiped down every night.

I love a clean, clear space. My kitchen isn't full of themed cookie jars or trinkets. I'm not sure when I decided that look wasn't for me, but I do know I cook and clean better when I'm not surrounded by stuff. That means taking stock of my big appliances—also known as dust collectors—and only keeping out the things I truly use on a regular basis. If you have a toaster oven, do you also need a toaster on the counter? This was an actual battle I had with my family—we just didn't have the space for both. In the end, the more versatile toaster oven won out.

I don't keep any food out on the counter. I precut and freeze all of my bread (it never goes in the fridge, where it will toughen and dry out). I have a three-tiered rack for veggies that shouldn't be refrigerated, like onions, garlic, tomatoes, and avocados. Hanging baskets and mesh bags are great for this purpose, too. But all fruit (except bananas) goes in the fridge or freezer.

I am a fresh flower person—and not just for Valentine's Day. I always keep a bouquet of some sort in the kitchen while I cook, even if it's just a few blooms from the supermarket or the yard and I'm the only one around to appreciate them. They're an instant mood lifter. Keeping a basil or mint plant on the counter has a similar calming effect on me—plus having fresh herbs at my fingertips (no rooting around in the crisper for that plastic clamshell of shriveled leaves) is a bonus when dinner could use an extra touch of freshness.

In my kitchen, I have only white plates. They just make life easier, and honestly, they make food look better, no matter the color. And I never have to struggle to find matching plates when we have extra guests. When I was getting married, everyone had china on their wedding registry. But if it makes an appearance twice a year, it's a miracle. I say put your money into different-colored napkins; they do wonders for your tablescape and you can't break them.

Watch my organizing hacks!

Watch my cleaning hacks!

HACK: Three Easy Ways to Rid Your Kitchen of After-Dinner Smells

1. Does your dishwasher still smell even after you've emptied it? Try this: Set a cup of vinegar on a saucer in an empty dishwasher and run it on a hot cycle. Or if you have a lemon, just cut it in half and toss both pieces on the top rack and run a cycle on hot!
2. A bowl of lemon wedges, white vinegar, and water works magic in your smelly microwave. Two minutes on high, and then let it steam.
3. To freshen up your kitchen sink, sprinkle the opening of your sink drain heavily with baking soda and follow that with some white vinegar. Wait for the fizzing to stop and then rinse it with hot water. Drop some lemon wedges and ice cubes in there and run your garbage disposal. I freeze old lemon leftovers to make ice cubes for just this occasion.

My Favorite Tools and Gadgets

As someone who has built a career out of trying to help others make life easier and get things done better, faster, and with a little flair, I'm constantly in the market for the best tools to aid in that effort. And that "research" often leads me to acquire more stuff than I have room for. So with that in mind, I don't recommend buying any wacky items that will only be used once (I'm talking to you, funnel cake maker!).

Here are some of the tools that truly come in handy for saving time and money in our house. Some are new discoveries; others are underused and underappreciated items that have been sitting there in the cupboard all along. Throughout these pages, you'll see how I call these tools into action. But if you don't already own them, have no fear—I'll give you a more conventional work-around.

6-quart slow cooker: While I have a couple friends who tossed their slow cookers when they bought an Instant Pot, I still prefer my 6-quart slow cooker for the one-pot meals I can start in the morning and forget about until dinnertime. But do what works for you!

Air fryer: Yep, it's a counter hog. But since it can produce crispy results without the grease in a fraction of the time a toaster or conventional oven requires, it remains in heavy rotation.

Panini press: Besides smashing bread and sandwiches, it works like magic for making a speedy quesadilla, frying bacon with less mess, or grilling burgers, chicken, fish, or veggies.

Waffle irons: I have several—both regular-size and mini. They're fast, inexpensive, and super easy to clean, and they take up little space. And they're good for so much more than waffles, from grilling sandwiches (like a panini press, with added crispy ridges), to "waffling" yesterday's mac and cheese or mashed potatoes.

Cuisinart Core 3-Cup Mini Chopper: It's just the right size for transforming stale chips into a quick crumb coating for fish or chicken (see Hack: Leftover Chips and Crackers, page 66) or for making my super simple Creamy Chimichurri Sauce (see page 28). And it's far less cumbersome and easier to wash than my 14-cup food processor, which I rarely use.

Electric hand mixer with storage case: I keep a KitchenAid stand mixer in a closet and haul it out only on rare occasions, like the holidays or when I want to whip up a large batch of cookies from scratch. But for most of my baking needs, a hand mixer works just as well and is far less of a hassle to deal with. It's much easier to store and fits great in a drawer.

Rimmed 13 x 18-inch (half-sheet) and 13 x 9-inch (quarter-sheet) baking sheets: These are the ultimate kitchen workhorses, and I have several of both. They're great for baking everything from roast meats to veggies to whole meals and can also sub for a pizza stone (see page 97) when turned upside down or a cupcake carrier with some painter's tape or even good ol' Scotch tape (see Hack: DIY Cupcake Carrier, page 257). I often double them up to keep things from burning on the bottom (see Hack: Avoiding Burnt Cupcake Bottoms, page 261).

Bundt pan (or tube pan): Even if you have no intentions of ever baking a pound cake, this pan is great for so many other things you wouldn't expect, such as roasting chickens rotisserie-style (see Bundt Pan Chicken and Vegetable Dinner, page 65), baking holiday stuffing for a pretty presentation (see Photogenic Turkey Dressing, page 206), or stripping kernels from ears of fresh corn in a hurry (see Hacks: Shucking and Stripping Corn, page 97).

7-inch santoku knife: If I had to invest in just one knife, this would be it! This incredibly versatile knife is basically the Japanese version of a chef's knife, and it's become my favorite knife of all time! It's the right size—not too big, not too short—and has a wide steel blade that slices, dices, and minces to perfection and a

fluted edge that prevents food from sticking. My trusty chef's knife still comes in handy for larger tasks like deboning meat (which I hardly ever do!), but the santoku practically does it all.

Rectangular cutting board with a slot: Although the slot is typically used as a handle for hanging, I've never actually hung a cutting board in my life, LOL! It's way more useful as a guide to save your veggies from ending up on the floor. After you've finished chopping, set the board on top of a bowl and slide the veggies or scraps through the slot with the back edge of your knife . . . straight into your bowl, the compost bin, or the trash can!

Crosshatch wire racks, aka cooling racks: Aside from baking and cooling, this is my secret weapon for the no-peel mashed potatoes that put me on the map: The Fluffiest Mashed Potatoes (page 132)! They're also great for draining grease, drying chocolate-covered treats, separating eggs, and preventing small vegetables or shrimp from slipping through the grill grates. And you can lay one on top of small bowls in the dishwasher to keep them from flipping.

Parchment paper, foil, and plastic wrap cutters: These may seem frivolous, but trust me, they will quickly become one of your favorite kitchen tools. No more tearing the plastic wrap at a weird angle or pulling out too much foil or struggling with the parchment—wondering who in the world ever got a clean cut from the flimsy paper box! You'll save money, too, because you'll be able to cut exactly the right amount the first time.

My Favorite Flavor Boosters

I won't go through the list of every staple in my kitchen because you probably already have so many of these things and know full well what to do with them. But I do want to call attention to my personal MVPs (most valuable players), the ones that are always there to step in to save me from buying a spice or condiment that I don't need to pull off a fabulous and flavorful feast, and the ones you will see throughout this book.

Salt and pepper: When it comes to cooking, there's nothing sexier than this dynamic duo! I'm a salt fanatic and use different kinds for different purposes. Over the past few years, I've adopted pink Himalayan salt—both fine and coarse—as my go-to salt. This ancient type of rock salt is less processed and has a slightly higher mineral content than table salt. But for baking and other recipes that call for specific measurements, any fine-grained salt will work. For seasoning food to taste, I'm a grinder gal who loves cranking coarse salt and fresh peppercorns as I go. And I'm a huge fan of Maldon sea salt flakes. I keep mine in a little marble salt cellar that lives on top of the stove and makes its way to the dinner table each night. Once you realize what this simple finishing salt can do to enhance the natural flavors of everything it touches (even my coffee!), it's an aha moment, like figuring out how to apply eyeliner for the first time! Buy a tub online and it will last you for years.

Garlic: There are two things my whole family agrees on. We're not fans of foods seasoned with too many spices. We are fans of garlic, though, and we'll take whatever form is available! We always have fresh bulbs that I'll often roast whole in the air fryer (see Roasted Garlic Spread, page 29), but I also keep a jar of minced garlic, (which I lovingly call jar-lic). There will be plenty of time for mincing garlic from scratch when I'm an empty nester! These days, I only chop up my own when I have the extra life minutes. I keep a bottle of garlic powder and a bag of frozen cloves handy when I need a shortcut.

Jarred pesto: This is one of my favorite convenient solutions for adding fresh herb flavor to foods when there's not a sprig in sight. There are many high-quality, ready-made pestos available that taste comparable to fresh. It makes a fantastic pizza sauce! It's especially good on my Half-Homemade California Summer Pizza (page 97), topping chicken or fish fillets (as in Pesto-Glazed Salmon with Roasted Asparagus and Cherry Tomatoes, page 74), and so much more.

Lemons and vinegar: A splash of acid—whether in the form of vinegar (I keep several varieties on hand) or citrus—can work wonders in salvaging an underwhelming dish. For me, fresh lemons are the most versatile, and they have the bonus of the fragrant zest, which adds an extra sparkle to fish, pasta, poultry, and veggies. And if I have more than I can use or they start to go south? They're one of my favorite natural cleaning supplies for taking the smell out of our garbage disposal, dishwasher, or microwave (see Hack: Three Easy Ways to Rid Your Kitchen of After-Dinner Smells, page 18).

Balsamic glaze: This thick, syrupy reduction of balsamic vinegar is tangy, sweet, and earthy all at once, great for drizzling straight from the bottle onto pizza, roast veggies, grilled meats . . . even vanilla ice cream or Greek yogurt.

Parmesan and pecorino Romano: In my kitchen, these umami-loaded hard cheeses are as much a seasoning as they are a protein source. Besides pasta and pizza, I grate them over roasted veggies (see Crispy, Cheesy, Smashed, and Roasted Broccoli, page 139) that even the kids will eat! Parmesan is cow's milk–based and is a little sweeter. Pecorino Romano is sheep's milk cheese and has a saltier taste. I prefer the latter, but they are interchangeable.

Tomato paste: It's amazing how a spoonful of super-concentrated tomato can transform a bland sauce or watery soup in seconds, both as a flavor booster and as a thickener! Although it's available in convenient tube form, cans are the better bargain for us because we go through so much of it. I freeze extra in ice cube trays and sometimes add garlic and other seasonings, and then drop them right into the pot of whatever I'm cooking: Tomato Flavor Bombs (see page 29).

Ro-Tel tomatoes and bottled salsa: I always keep a can of these zesty tomatoes and chiles to add to chili, casseroles, cheese dip, or anything that could use a Tex-Mex kick. If your market doesn't carry them, your favorite salsa will work great! You can also add a tiny can of mild green chiles to a can of chopped tomatoes to make your own version of Ro-Tel.

Tamari: This Japanese sauce is as savory and versatile as its more popular cousin, soy sauce. But I prefer it because it has a somewhat smoother, richer, less salty taste, and it's gluten-free. I use it to marinate meats, season vegetables, whisk into salad dressings, and make my own Teriyaki Sauce (page 29) for glazing and drizzling.

How I Stock My Pantry

Cluttered cabinets can be the Achilles' heel of any well-meaning home cook. I'm always amazed when I watch those cooking shows with fully stocked pantries where the contestants somehow know everything that's in them and where to find exactly what they need to complete their dish before the buzzer goes off. My solution is a lot simpler: I curate my kitchen just like the fashion gals do with their closets: taking regular inventory and seeing what's in there that needs to be used up or purged.

Old food is tossed or composted on Monday. I plan my grocery lists and recipe choices around the ingredients I have on hand and the foods my family will eat. In my fridge, I have a designated area for leftovers so they don't get lost or forgotten. I'm big on giving staples, such as ketchup and ranch dressing, their own "spots" so I'll know at a glance when we're running low.

When choosing my products, I read labels and mostly steer clear of products full of weird ingredients I know—or at least suspect—aren't great for us. I buy grass-fed beef and pasture-raised eggs, and I don't mind paying a few extra pennies for an organic product without the pesticides and other additives over a cheaper version. I find that our family feels better when we eat this way, and honestly, fresh just tastes better.

But I don't obsess about these things! Here again, I go by my 90/10 rule of health-conscious eating most of the time while cutting all of us some slack now and then.

Decluttering the Spice Drawer

How old is the oldest spice in your cabinet? Mine is a jar of bay leaves, which literally takes me years to use! For years, I'll bet I wasn't using half of the spices we'd all been told we "needed" to have on hand. Then one day, feeling exhausted from rummaging through that overflowing drawer of rarely used bottles for one-off recipes I never made again, I decided it was time for a purge. I started buying in small batches, as fresh spices are the best and go bad (or at least lose their potency) fast.

Nowadays, I buy only four seasonings in bulk: salt, pepper, garlic powder, and taco seasoning mix. Having packets of dry ranch seasoning and onion soup mix on hand also saves me from buying more spices than I need. And then there's Magic Seasoning (page 28)! This little blend is not groundbreaking by any means: It's four parts salt, one part ground pepper, and one part garlic powder. That's it! But having it on hand will transform your dishes fast.

Some Notes About Ingredients

Salt: As previously mentioned, my go-to salt for any recipe calling for specific measurements is fine pink Himalayan salt (see page 22), but any fine salt you have on hand will do.

Butter: I use salted butter for everything. For one thing, the salt acts as a preservative, and it can stay out on the counter for up to a couple of days; unsalted should stay out for no more than a few hours. And it just makes everything taste better. I love Kerrygold butter.

Oils: Avocado oil is my go-to for most of my cooking mainly because of its high smoke point. Like olive oil, it gets high marks for its health benefits, and it has a mild flavor and creamy texture that allows other flavors to shine through, making it extremely versatile in cooking, baking, salad-making . . . you name it! But if you don't have it, it's interchangeable with any neutral oil. I use extra-virgin olive oil for dressing salads and when I want a more pronounced flavor in recipes. In general, I don't heat olive oil over 300°F because of its lower smoke point.

Nonstick cooking spray: Avocado oil spray (Chosen Foods is great) is my top choice for greasing pans. Unlike other sprays, it's free of propellants and additives. And with its neutral taste and 500°F smoke point, it's great for spritzing on veggies and other foods before roasting, grilling, sautéing, or air-frying. It's especially handy for baking cakes. Once I've sprayed my pans, I shake in a little flour and tap out the excess.

Eggs: I always use large, pasture-raised eggs, although the size really doesn't matter (except for baking).

How to Be a Savvy Shopper

You won't have to schlep all over town hunting down any of the ingredients called for in this book, as they can all be found at any supermarket. But to get the biggest bang for my buck, I find that one stop just doesn't do the trick, so I shop multiple stores. I start at the most affordable one and work my way up so that I'm only buying what I truly need at the high-end ones, which have items that no one else is carrying.

It takes some preplanning at first to work these stops into your routes so you're not spending all of your grocery savings on gas. But eventually it becomes an easy habit you don't really think about. I realize this strategy doesn't necessarily make sense for all lifestyles or households—say if you don't spend that much time in your car or you're only shopping for one or two. But here's what works for me that may help you craft a frugal plan to fit your own needs.

Some General Tips for Cutting Your Grocery Bills

Start with an organized shopping list. There are some super-handy smartphone apps out there to help you manage grocery lists between multiple stores, many with other bells and whistles like tracking when pantry supplies are running low and matching coupons with local weekly store ads. I have a note in my phone where I keep a running grocery list. Whether you do it the high-tech way or old-school way with pen and paper, the first rule of thumb is to organize by store aisle to avoid running back and forth and seeing more temptations. To help you start your own, I've shared my most basic checklist—which covers most of the recipes in this book!—in a printable form on my website.

Avoid the weekend and after-work crowds. Tuesdays and Wednesdays are typically the best days to shop for the biggest savings. On Wednesdays, most stores are still going to honor the coupons from the week before. Go before folks get off work if you can, as some stores change pricing throughout the day! And if you go in the morning when stores are less crowded, you'll be less tempted to make rash decisions.

Keep walking past the front of the store. That's where the pricey stuff tends to be. The deals are more likely to be found at the middle and back of the store.

Walk past the samples. You're up to 65 percent more likely to buy that product if you try it.

Scan the shelves top to bottom. The most expensive items at the grocery store are usually at eye level. You can save up to 80 percent by reaching for items on the higher and lower shelves!

Learn to decipher price tags. This can take some research (Google is your friend here), as every store is different. Take Costco as one example: If the price ends in .97, it's on clearance. An asterisk means the item won't be restocked, so if it's a product you like, you might want to stock up. If it ends in .88, that means the item may have been returned or slightly damaged, stocks are running low, or the manager is anxious to move inventory. And if the tag is green, it's organic.

Shop after the holidays. Don't overlook the items that can easily be repurposed for the next holiday. For example: Halloween candy can become fantastic Thanksgiving treats; if you just toss the bats and ghosts, the coloring is pretty darn close. Christmas candies can be divided into red and silver for Valentine's Day, and the green and gold can be used for St. Patrick's Day. Memorial Day and Fourth of July are pretty much the same, so stock up anytime you see these holiday-specific treats on sale!

You can also save by using self checkout. It helps you stick to your list.

Warehouse Clubs

I have memberships to both Costco and Sam's Club because each has its own set of pluses and minuses. Both offer instant savings and relatively similar coupon books, and each has the staple rotisserie chicken for a crazy low price. Although Sam's Club boasts better prices overall, Costco makes up for its slightly higher costs with better item selection and product quality.

The difference in pricing is also reflected in the ambience. Costco has better lighting and nicer displays, giving off the vibe of a more elevated shopping experience. Sam's Club is more bare-bones, telling you that you're likely getting the rock-bottom lowest pricing, as they aren't focused on frills.

Overall, I've found Costco is better for organic produce and baked goods. And in a pinch, their prepared meals are delicious, but they're pricier than if you made them yourself. Sam's Club has better pricing on kids' items like diapers and accessories. If you're a team parent or need to provide snacks for games or the classroom, again, Sam's Club is a better deal. Another advantage over Costco: Curbside pickup that allows you to avoid the long lines as well as a "Scan and Go" option in the store's app that gives you a running total as you shop. Any store that offers pickup will likely save you money because you will only order what you need and won't get caught up in impulse shopping while walking around the store.

Check out my basic checklist—which covers most of the recipes in this book!

Magic Seasoning + 4 Other DIY Secret Weapons

I'm not above taking the easy way out with a ready-made blend or sauce, but I do have a handful of little concoctions that are so simple, versatile, and economical they're well worth the extra few minutes it takes to whip them up myself. Hardly a day goes by that I don't reach for my Magic Seasoning, as will soon be clear to you when you read my recipes. The others here are great to have on hand when whatever we're about to eat could use just a little something extra. I show how I use them in some of these pages.

Magic Seasoning

MAKES 1½ CUPS

When I was growing up, there wasn't a restaurant meal my mom, Norma Jean, didn't comment on, giving it a pass or fail grade based on its seasoning level. She's always had the Midas touch when it comes to cooking, and now we can, too, thanks to what I call Magic Seasoning. Here is the DIY blend my mom gives an A+. The magic lies in the simplicity!

- 1 cup fine salt
- ¼ cup ground black pepper
- ¼ cup garlic powder

1. Combine the salt, pepper, and garlic powder in a jar and mix well. Store with a tight-fitting lid. Use in any savory dish!

Creamy Chimichurri Sauce

MAKES ABOUT ½ CUP

If you're looking for a wow moment with little effort, this herbal Argentinian sauce is it! It's like putting mascara on your lashes—the impact is huge, quick, and immediate. Chimichurri is typically slathered over Marinated and Grilled Steak (page 210), but it's also great over roasted vegetables or as a marinade for any protein. I make mine in my little food processor rather than chopping everything by hand. Since parsley is relatively cheap and sold in bunches way too big for us to go through before it dies, I will happily double and triple this recipe and freeze extras in ice cube trays to use as needed.

- 1 packed cup parsley leaves
- 2 to 3 teaspoons chopped garlic
- 2 teaspoons dried oregano
- 2 tablespoons red or white wine vinegar
- ½ teaspoon salt
- ⅛ teaspoon black pepper
- ¼ teaspoon red pepper flakes
- ⅓ cup extra-virgin olive oil

1. Place the parsley, garlic, oregano, vinegar, salt, pepper, and red pepper flakes in a blender or food processor and pulse a few times.
2. With the machine on low, drizzle in the oil and blend until smooth or to the desired consistency. (Some like it coarse.)
3. Transfer to a container and store, tightly covered, in the refrigerator until ready to use, for up to 2 weeks. Or pour the chimichurri sauce into an ice cube tray, freeze it, and pop the frozen cubes into a freezer-safe storage bag or container for up to 3 months. Thaw the night before in the refrigerator before using.

Roasted Garlic Spread

MAKES ABOUT ½ CUP

Are you a fan of creamy roasted garlic? If you haven't tried it, add this one to your list immediately! It looks super fancy but is so low lift and fast, you won't believe it. I may spread it on whatever we're eating that night—steak, chicken, veggies, bread. Or I'll mash it up and mix it into salad dressings, sauces, sandwich spreads, or dips. Kid 2 likes to squeeze the cloves directly into her mouth!

- 4 garlic bulbs
- Big pinch of flaky salt, or whatever salt you have
- 4 teaspoons avocado oil or olive oil, or more if needed

1. Preheat the air fryer or oven to 400°F. Remove the outer paper layer of the garlic, leaving just enough peel to hold the garlic cloves together.
2. Cut the tips off the garlic bulbs, exposing the cloves. Sprinkle with salt, drizzle with oil, wrap with foil, and place in the air fryer or oven, cut-side up.
3. Air-fry for 25 minutes or bake in the oven for 50 to 60 minutes, until very soft. Let cool then unwrap the foil and peel the cloves.
4. To store, place the peeled cloves in a jar. Top with oil, cover tightly with a lid, and store in the fridge for up to 2 weeks.

Teriyaki Sauce

MAKES 1 CUP

This salty-sweet, umami-rich sauce is traditionally used as a glaze for grilled meats, but a drizzle can add zing to most anything, such as my Egg Roll Bowls (page 158) or Teriyaki Salmon and Cauliflower "Rice" Bowl (page 161). My version uses gluten-free tamari and monk fruit–based brown sugar. But feel free to go with any soy sauce–like product or sweetener you prefer. My version of teriyaki sauce is on the thinner side; to make it into a glaze, reduce the sauce until you've achieved your desired consistency.

- ¾ cup tamari or low-sodium soy sauce
- ¼ cup brown monk fruit sweetener (I use Lakanto) or brown sugar
- 1 tablespoon chopped fresh garlic or 2 teaspoons bottled minced garlic
- 1 tablespoon apple cider vinegar
- ¼ teaspoon ground ginger

1. Mix the tamari, sweetener, garlic, vinegar, and ginger in a small saucepan.
2. Bring to a boil and then reduce the heat to a simmer for about 5 minutes, or until it coats the back of a spoon. (It will thicken a bit more as it cools.) Store in an airtight container in the fridge for up to 2 weeks.

Tomato Flavor Bombs

I used to store half-used tomato paste cans in the fridge, where they'd linger until they got too old to eat. Then I figured out how to turn them into flavor bombs! Drop tomato paste by tablespoonfuls into freezer ice cube trays, add ¼ teaspoon chopped garlic to each cube, and sprinkle with dried basil, oregano, or Italian seasoning. Freeze and then pop them into a bag, label, and store in the freezer for up to 3 months. Use in pasta sauces, soups, stews, eggs, or anything that could use a boost of intense tomato flavor!

Weekdays and Weeknights

CHAPTER 1

Healthy Starts for Busy Days

I've been pretty focused on healthy eating for as long as I've been living in LA. It wasn't easy when I first landed here, thinking breakfast was biscuits and gravy with an ice-cold Coke! But this town has long since opened my eyes and made it easier to make better choices, and now it's a way of life. I use an Oura Ring to make sure I'm getting my steps in and lift weights periodically. But the biggest game changer has been dialing in my eating habits. I've found that by sticking mostly to a low-carb diet with enough protein at every meal, I can easily control my portions and won't be tempted to snack after dinner. This routine begins first thing in the morning, even during the most hectic weeks when my family is going in all different directions and at different speeds, and we typically fend for ourselves. I try to keep the kitchen stocked at all times with easy, healthy options for breakfast—from the on-the-go sips and bites that keep me full until the next meal to super-fast, low-sugar breakfasts even the kids can whip up before dashing out the door.

My Favorite Detox Smoothie

SERVES 1

This is my ultra-fast and satisfying way to start the day with a serving of fruit and veggies and a boost of protein—plus chocolate! And there are so many ways to customize it, even for the kids. For myself, I add some of the nutrition-loaded extras I keep on hand for myself that would never get past my kids' lips. It's amazing how a ripe banana or a scoop of peanut butter can hide the taste of just about anything! To avoid little green bits giving away your secret, place the spinach in the blender first along with the water and give it a few pulses before adding the other ingredients. Use frozen fruit if you can; if you use fresh, you may want to toss in a handful of ice, though the texture may be on the slushy side.

- Handful of baby spinach leaves
- 1 cup water
- 1 ripe banana, preferably frozen
- ½ cup frozen blueberries
- 1 scoop (about 1 ounce) chocolate or vanilla protein powder (see Note)
- 2 tablespoons hemp hearts or 1 to 2 tablespoons nut butter
- Hearty dash of ground cinnamon
- Handful of ice, optional

ADD-INS, OPTIONAL

- 2 tablespoons sea moss gel (I like Erewhon cosmic berry)
- 1 tablespoon chia seeds
- 1 teaspoon bee pollen granules

1. Place the spinach leaves and water in a (preferably) high-speed blender and pulse a few times to puree.
2. Add the banana, blueberries, protein powder, hemp hearts, cinnamon, ice (if using), and whatever add-ins you wish. Blend until smooth, 1 or 2 minutes, and then pour into a glass and drink up (or pour into a tumbler for the road).

NOTE

I keep containers of flavored protein powders on hand for a convenient way to keep me full on busy days when I may miss a balanced meal—plus, they taste good! Protein powders made of whey, egg, or plants typically contain all the essential amino acids that make them a complete protein source and are best for strength-building and muscle repair. But I prefer collagen protein powders. (Be Well by Kelly is one of my favorite brands.) Collagen (derived from animal sources) is an incomplete source of protein but is the best choice for healthy joints and bones, smooth skin, and strong nails and hair. Collagen powders can be used interchangeably with other protein powders in recipes, but all powders have different tastes and textures. Be sure to read labels carefully and do your own research to know what you're getting!

HACK: Mocha Coffee

Some days, breakfast is just not in the cards for me, but I need to have my morning coffee no matter what! I have a protein-boosting trick for transforming that cup of courage into something more satisfying and substantial than a wake-up call. I'll stir in a scoop of chocolate collagen powder, a few drops of liquid stevia, some Nutpods French Vanilla creamer, and a pinch of flaky sea salt (to take off the bitter edge)—and it's delicious! If I have an extra minute, I'll blend it up with my handy little milk frother to make it taste extra creamy and, if need be, pour it into a thermos to carry with me in the car.

Energy Muffins

MAKES 12

This is my go-to muffin recipe! I keep a batch in the freezer for whenever I need a boost. These low-carb, fiber- and protein-rich muffins aren't very sweet or attractive, but somehow, they win you over! So when you pull them out of the oven, if they look uber-healthy, you've nailed 'em. I originally found this nugget in an awesome cookbook called *Make Ahead Paleo* by Tammy Credicott. She calls her version Breakfast Muffins, but I've tweaked them, replacing the sugar with a mashed banana and just a tablespoon of liquid stevia simple syrup (such as NuNaturals brand), which is about eight times as sweet as regular sugar. It's great for mixing into drinks, pouring over pancakes, baking, and more. But it's quite expensive and can be hard to find. Luckily, I found that ½ cup of zero-calorie monk fruit brown sugar makes an excellent sub without extra tinkering. (The same amount of regular brown sugar could be used if sugar is less of an issue for you.) Top with almond butter and it'll feel like you're eating a breakfast cupcake! If you're feeling fancy, try a little cream cheese with apple butter or preserves on top.

- 1 small very ripe banana (about ⅓ cup mashed)
- 6 large eggs
- 1 tablespoon stevia simple syrup, ½ cup monk fruit brown sugar, or ½ cup brown sugar
- 2 teaspoons vanilla extract
- ¾ cup almond flour
- ⅓ cup coconut flour
- 1 teaspoon ground cinnamon
- ½ teaspoon baking soda
- ½ teaspoon ground cloves
- ½ teaspoon ground ginger
- Pinch of sea salt
- 1 cup finely shredded carrots
- 1 cup finely shredded zucchini
- ¼ cup raw shelled pumpkin seeds, sunflower seeds, or whatever seed you have
- ¼ cup chopped walnuts

1. Preheat the oven to 350°F. Line a 12-cup muffin tin with paper liners. (These muffins are quite fragile, so greasing the wells alone may not be enough to prevent them from sticking.)
2. Mash the banana in a large bowl. Add the eggs, stevia simple syrup, and vanilla, and mix well.
3. Mix the almond flour, coconut flour, cinnamon, baking soda, cloves, ginger, and salt in a medium bowl. Add the dry ingredients to the wet ingredients and mix well with a wooden spoon.
4. Press out the excess moisture from the carrots and zucchini with a paper towel. Then fold the carrots, zucchini, pumpkin seeds, and walnuts into the mixture and mix until just combined.
5. Divide the batter evenly among the prepared muffin cups, filling each about three-quarters of the way up the liner. Bake for 25 to 30 minutes, until a cake tester inserted in the center comes out clean.

Storage Tip

Store the muffins in an airtight container for up to 3 days in the refrigerator or wrap them individually in plastic wrap and freeze for up to 3 months. Let them thaw in the fridge overnight or on the countertop for an hour . . . maybe even less. Or wrap each muffin in a damp paper towel and microwave on low power in 30-second intervals until thawed. Take care not to overdo it as they dry out easily. Eat within 2 days for maximum freshness.

HACK: Speed-Ripen an Unripe Banana

What do you do if the only banana you have to work with is unripe and too hard to mash? You can do the old trick of wrapping it up in a paper bag to speed the ripening—it's even faster if you slip in a slice of apple. Since that might take a day or so, here's an easy solution if you want a ripe banana now: Simply place it on a parchment-lined pan and roast it in a 350°F oven with the skin on for 10 minutes or longer, checking every few minutes to see if it's soft enough. The peel will blacken and the banana may be too mushy for slicing, but it's perfect for folding into a batter for baking! If you want something even faster, prick the banana all over with a fork, set it on a paper towel, and microwave it in 30-second intervals until it reaches your desired softness. It won't be as sweet as if you do the oven method but will work in a pinch.

Nutty No-Bake Protein Balls

MAKES 30 TO 36

This is the answer to my late-morning or afternoon voice that whispers, "I want a candy bar!" These make-ahead protein balls taste better than a Snickers, IMO, and are definitely better for you. Plus, they freeze like a dream. Sit a couple out for a few minutes or pop them in the microwave for 15 seconds to soften just a little. These are great for road trips and lunch boxes, too! You can make them your own . . . add butterscotch or vanilla chips, cut back on the nuts, or add more coconut. You really can't mess these up.

- 1 cup raw cashews
- ½ cup raw whole almonds
- ½ cup raw walnut or pecan halves
- ½ teaspoon salt
- 1 cup shredded unsweetened coconut, divided
- ¾ cup smooth peanut butter or almond butter (see Note)
- ⅓ cup honey
- 2 tablespoons chia seeds or seeds of choice
- 1 teaspoon vanilla extract
- ½ teaspoon ground cinnamon
- ½ cup mini chocolate chips, optional

1. Line a large, rimmed baking sheet with parchment paper.
2. Place the nuts, the salt, and half the coconut in a food processor and pulse 3 or 4 times, until the mixture resembles coarse crumbs.
3. Place the peanut butter and honey in a large, microwave-safe bowl and microwave the mixture on 50 percent power for 30 seconds until slightly warm, just long enough to make it easier to mix with the dry ingredients, and then stir. Add the nut/coconut mixture, the remaining coconut, and the chia seeds, vanilla, and cinnamon. If the mixture is still warm, let it cool completely and then mix in the chocolate chips, if using.
4. Scoop heaping tablespoons of the mixture onto the baking sheet. Roll each portion into a tight ball between your palms and place the baking sheet in the refrigerator until chilled and firm, about 30 minutes.

Note

If using natural peanut butter, stir well to emulsify before using.

Storage Tip

Place the balls in an airtight container and store in the refrigerator for up to 2 weeks or in the freezer for up to 3 months. Allow them to sit out for a few minutes to thaw slightly and eat chilled. (They're also good at room temperature.)

Mini Waffle and Sausage Breakfast on a Stick

MAKES 18

I grew up in the "anything on a stick" era! It's amazing how something so basic can turn into something special just by offering it on a stick, right? Corn dogs, popsicles, kebabs—so why not breakfast? Here's where my mini waffle iron comes to the rescue. This recipe works with any waffle batter and any type of sausage, and—if you make the batter the night before—it's ready in less than five minutes! You can make these keto, low-carb, high-protein, gluten-free, dairy-free, and even vegan! The possibilities are endless. This is an easy, kid-friendly way to serve utensil-free waffles for a crowd or to scale down for a fast breakfast on the go. Follow the basic batter recipe here or use a mix and follow the package directions.

- 2 cups all-purpose flour
- 2 tablespoons sugar
- 1 tablespoon plus 1 teaspoon baking powder
- ½ teaspoon salt
- 2 large eggs
- 1½ cups milk (any kind)
- ⅓ cup (⅔ stick) melted butter (cooled to room temperature)
- 1 teaspoon vanilla extract
- Nonstick cooking spray or melted butter, for greasing
- 18 cooked sausage patties (pork, chicken, or plant-based), thawed if frozen
- 18 wooden coffee stir sticks
- Melted butter and maple syrup, for dipping (in separate bowls or mixed together)

1. Preheat your waffle iron according to the manufacturer's instructions.
2. Whisk the flour, sugar, baking powder, and salt in a medium bowl. Whisk the eggs, milk, butter, and vanilla in a large bowl.
3. Stir the dry mixture into the wet mixture until just combined, taking care not to overmix. If the batter seems too thick (it should be pourable), stir in a little more milk.
4. Spray your preheated waffle iron with cooking spray.
5. Insert a stick into the edge of each sausage through the center to the other side. Dip a patty into the batter and then set it in the waffle iron.
6. Close the lid and cook according to the waffle iron manufacturer's instructions, or until golden brown.
7. Repeat steps 5 and 6 to make the remaining waffles, spraying with more cooking spray between batches to prevent sticking.
8. Serve with bowls of melted butter and maple syrup for dipping.

Breakfast Sandwiches on the Go

MAKES 12

If you're tired of grabbing the same protein bar in the morning but don't have time to cook breakfast (who does?), my make-ahead Egg McMuffin dupes are the solution! Make them by the dozen and freeze. Just toss them in the microwave on a busy morning and eat in the car.

- Nonstick cooking spray or butter, for greasing
- 12 large eggs
- Salt and pepper
- 12 English muffins
- ½ cup (1 stick) melted butter
- 12 slices cheese of choice (such as American, cheddar, or Monterey Jack)
- 12 slices cooked bacon or meat of choice (such as Canadian bacon, sliced ham, cooked sausage patties, or plant-based meat substitute)

1. Preheat the oven to 350°F. Coat a 12-cup muffin pan with cooking spray and crack an egg into each cup. Sprinkle each with a little salt and pepper. Bake for about 15 minutes, or until the whites are opaque.
2. Meanwhile, split the English muffins in half, lay them out open-faced on two baking sheets, and brush with butter. Bake for 5 to 7 minutes, until golden brown.
3. Remove the muffin pan and baking sheets from the oven. Lay a slice of bacon on the bottom half of each muffin and then top with a piece of cheese. Scoop out each egg with a spoon and place one on top of each piece of cheese. Then cover with the top halves of the muffins.

Storage Tip

Wrap each muffin tightly in plastic wrap, place in a freezer-safe bag, and freeze for up to 3 months. When ready to eat, remove the plastic wrap from a muffin, place it on a microwave-safe plate, cover it with a damp paper towel, and microwave on high for 1 minute, or until heated through.

You can also reheat the muffins in an air fryer set at 325°F for 3 or 4 minutes. I like to break mine open when I do it this way, which allows the cheese to get bubbly and the edges of the muffin to get extra crispy.

Overnight Peanut Butter Jar Chia Pudding

SERVES 1

Are you the type of person who scrapes the very last bit of peanut butter out of a jar? If you're like me and don't like wasting an ounce, this hack is for you! My husband, Scooter, cannot wrap his head around this snack, but trust me, it's delicious! It's my take on overnight oats but without the oats, with a few big spoonfuls of teeny nutrition-packed chia seeds to give it a pudding-like consistency when shaken up with milk. Easy, low-carb, and full of fiber.

- One almost-empty 12- to 16-ounce peanut butter jar (see Note)
- Handful of fresh or frozen berries (roughly crushed for a more colorful pudding)
- ½ cup milk (any kind), plus a few more tablespoons, if needed
- 2 tablespoons chia seeds

ADD-INS, OPTIONAL

- Chopped nuts
- Pinch of ground cinnamon
- Stevia or sweetener of choice
- Sunflower or pumpkin seeds

1. Fill the peanut butter jar with berries, milk, chia seeds, and any optional add-ins. Mix with a fork to distribute the berries and chia seeds throughout the milk.
2. Cover with the lid, shake well, and refrigerate overnight. Eat with a spoon, straight from the jar.

Watch me make this!

Note

If you don't want to wait until your peanut butter jar is empty, simply place 1 or 2 tablespoons of peanut butter in a clean, empty 12- to 16-ounce jar and proceed with step 1.

Lemon Chia Pudding

SERVES 1

When I was little, I loved the lemon pie filling my mom, Norma Jean, made so much that I couldn't wait for it to cool down! I remember taking a spoonful of the thick and still-warm filling and eating it just like a lollipop. This chia pudding has all of the same flavors and is perfect for breakfast. Don't spend time focusing on the chia seeds, which act as a thickener and make you feel full. You'll end up eating this one because you love it. The protein and fiber and other healthy stuff will just be a bonus! Make it the night before as a breakfast—or an afternoon pick-me-up—and it's ready when you are the next day.

- 1 cup macadamia nut milk, almond milk, or other milk of choice
- 10 drops liquid stevia or 1 tablespoon maple syrup, honey, or agave (or to taste)
- Zest and juice of 1 lemon (see Hack)
- ¼ cup chia seeds
- Fresh or frozen berries or chopped fruit (such as kiwi or mango), for topping, optional

1. Mix the milk, stevia, lemon zest, and lemon juice in a medium bowl. Add the chia seeds and whisk well. Alternatively, place all the ingredients in a pint-size jar with a tight-fitting lid and shake vigorously.
2. Let the mixture set for about 15 minutes, until it begins to gel. Then give it another stir or shake to break up any clumps, cover, and refrigerate for at least 4 hours, or up to 6 days.
3. Add any toppings right before eating.

HACK: Juicing a Lemon

Here's the easiest way ever to juice a lemon that requires only a wooden or metal skewer or a chopstick. Roll the lemon around the counter to soften it up a bit for easier squeezing. Then stick the sharp end of a skewer into one end of the lemon, about two inches into the peel, down to the pulp. Remove the skewer, place the hole over a bowl, and start squeezing—no cutting required and no seeds to fish out! The whole lemon will still be intact for easy zesting (I use a microplane). If you only need a splash, wrap up the lemon in plastic and stick it in the fridge until you need it again.

Make-Ahead Fill-You-Up Oatmeal

SERVES 4

I love oatmeal! Truly, I do. And while it's pretty healthy as is, I grew up eating cream of wheat, cream of rice—all the hot, creamy cereals out there. In fact, I was more of a hot cereal kid than a cold one. I would add sugar and butter to my cream of wheat and then let it get cold so I could cut it into squares—it was basically sweet polenta! When I moved to California, cream of wheat wasn't a big thing, but oatmeal was. I had seen someone online putting frozen riced cauliflower in their oatmeal to sneak a veggie in and was inspired. I added protein powder, vanilla, cinnamon—all the flavorful things to disguise any cauliflower flavor. To shrink the prep time and cleanup to practically nothing, I make a batch and divide it among baggies I can reach for in the freezer.

2 cups water

One 12-ounce bag riced cauliflower

1 cup rolled oats (or oats with seeds and nuts added, such as Trader Joe's)

4 scoops (about 4 ounces) vanilla protein powder

1 teaspoon vanilla extract, optional

½ teaspoon ground cinnamon, optional

Pinch of salt, or to taste

TOPPINGS, OPTIONAL

Fresh berries

Chopped fruit

Chopped nuts

Raisins

1. Bring the water to a boil in a medium saucepan. Add the cauliflower and oats and cook, stirring occasionally, until the liquid is absorbed, about 5 minutes.
2. Stir in the protein powder one scoop at a time, mixing well after each addition. Stir in the vanilla and cinnamon, if using, and salt.
3. Serve immediately with toppings of choice. Or to enjoy later, divide the oatmeal among four freezer bags, cool thoroughly, and then seal and refrigerate for up to 4 days, or freeze for up to 4 months (see Storage Tip).

Storage Tip

To freeze and reheat: Press the bags flat and freeze. (When pressed flat, they're much easier to stack and store in the freezer, and they thaw much more quickly.) To thaw, run the bag under hot water and then pour it into a bowl and finish heating in the microwave. Garnish as desired.

Low-Carb Protein Pancakes

SERVES 1

If you're craving pancakes but want a lower-carb option, these are fantastic. A single-serve blender or handheld blender works great for whipping these ingredients into a smooth batter in less than a minute. But if you don't have one, you can mix them in a bowl by hand using quick-cooking or instant oats. They'll be a little lumpier, which I kinda like, and will taste just as great! Once you top them with some butter or my favorite—peanut butter—these read like pancakes, but unlike regular ones, these are packed with protein.

1 large egg

2 tablespoons cottage cheese

2 tablespoons rolled oats (use quick-cooking or instant if mixing by hand)

1 tablespoon protein powder (see Note, page 35)

¼ teaspoon baking powder

¼ teaspoon ground cinnamon

¼ teaspoon grated lemon zest

¼ teaspoon vanilla extract

⅛ teaspoon salt

Few drops of liquid stevia (or sweetener of choice)

Splash of milk (enough to make a batter)

1 tablespoon fresh blueberries, plus more for serving, optional

1 to 2 teaspoons neutral oil

Butter, peanut butter, or other nut butter, for serving, optional

1. Place the egg, cottage cheese, oats, protein powder, baking powder, cinnamon, lemon zest, vanilla, salt, and stevia in a blender or medium bowl. Blend for a minute or so (or beat with a fork), adding enough milk to make a batter (it's okay if it's lumpy). Stir in the blueberries, if using.
2. Heat a large skillet or griddle over medium heat. Add just enough oil to coat the skillet.
3. Drop the batter by large spoonfuls onto the hot skillet and cook until the bottoms brown and bubbles begin to form on the surface, about 1 minute. Flip and cook on the second side until lightly browned, about 30 seconds longer. Transfer to a plate and serve warm with butter, if using, or your preferred topping.

90-Second Gluten-Free English Muffin in a Mug (for One)

SERVES 1

Cutting carbs can be a challenge in a family of bread-eaters, especially on mornings when everyone wants toast. I was thrilled to discover this quickie hack that doesn't involve buying a special loaf just for me. Toasted, this is an incredible body double for an English muffin. For a low-carb topping, add a smear of nut butter instead of jam or honey. It's a good protein boost as well.

- ⅓ cup almond flour
- 1 large egg
- ½ teaspoon baking powder
- 1 tablespoon salted butter, melted

TOPPINGS, OPTIONAL

- Sliced strawberries
- Maple syrup

1. Mix the almond flour, egg, and baking powder with a fork in a small bowl until it forms a thick batter.
2. Pour the melted butter into a ramekin or large mug. Stir in the batter and smooth the top.
3. Microwave on high for 90 seconds. Carefully remove the muffin from the mug by running a knife around the edges. It will pop right out and be hot. Cut in half and toast or eat as is. Top with strawberries and syrup if desired.

Nut-Free Option

Combine 1 large egg, 2 tablespoons coconut flour, 2 tablespoons milk (any kind), and ⅛ teaspoon baking powder in a small bowl, mixing with a fork until smooth. Then proceed with Step 2.

PORTED FROM MEXICO
HOLULA
HOT SAUCE
RIGINAL
FL OZ (150 mL)

Pesto-Feta Egg Sandwich

SERVES 1

If you want to feel like you're cooking without the pressure of cooking, this is it. Kid 2 gets the credit for this one. She took the viral pesto egg craze to the next level with four simple ingredients: pesto, egg, feta, and toast! The cheese and pesto melt together like a gooey blanket around the egg. But when you top it with toast and flip it, it instantly turns into one of the best breakfast sandwiches I've ever had. Add a little hot sauce or Parmesan cheese before you fold it for a little something extra.

1 large slice sourdough bread
2 tablespoons prepared pesto
1 large egg, lightly beaten
2 tablespoons crumbled feta
Few shakes of hot sauce, optional
Spoonful of grated Parmesan, optional

1. Toast the sourdough bread and cut it in half.
2. Spoon the pesto into a small nonstick skillet and set the lid next to the skillet.
3. Turn the heat to medium and swirl the pan to coat with the pesto. Cook until the oil in the pesto starts to bubble, about 1 minute, and then pour the beaten egg on top, sprinkle with feta, and top immediately with the two bread halves.
4. Cook for a minute or two, until the egg is set. Grabbing the lid with one hand and the skillet handle with the other, slide the egg/pesto/toast combo onto the lid. Flip it back into the skillet so the egg is facing up, and let it cook for a few seconds more.
5. Top with hot sauce and/or Parmesan, if using. Then fold it over so the two bread halves form a sandwich. Press it down with a spatula, transfer to a plate, and dig in!

Mediterranean Scramble for Two

SERVES 2

If eggs are happening on a weekday, they must happen fast! This is my super quick remake of a Greek omelet using some leftover tidbits from the fridge. Instead of fiddling with the omelet flipping, I just sauté the veggies first and pour the eggs right on top and start stirring to scramble. (In fact, I often sauté this veggie combo for dinner as a side dish, and if there are extras, I can have the first two steps done before I begin!) While the eggs cook, I'll brew the coffee and pop some bread in the toaster or air fryer—high-fiber, gluten-free for me, always sourdough for Scoot. Easy peasy!

- 1 tablespoon avocado oil
- ½ small onion, chopped
- Salt and pepper
- Drizzle of balsamic vinegar
- Drizzle of Worcestershire sauce (I use gluten-free)
- Handful of cherry tomatoes, diced
- Handful of spinach
- 1½ teaspoons butter
- 4 large eggs, well beaten
- 2 to 3 tablespoons crumbled feta

1. Heat the oil in a medium nonstick skillet over medium heat and swirl to coat the bottom. Add the onion, season with a little salt and pepper, and sauté until tender, 4 or 5 minutes. Add a generous drizzle of vinegar and Worcestershire sauce, mixing to coat.
2. Stir in the tomatoes and cook until softened, 2 or 3 minutes. Top with the spinach and allow it to wilt for a minute or so. Then add the butter and stir in to melt.
3. Pour in the eggs and cook, stirring gently with a spatula to scramble, until desired firmness is achieved, 3 to 5 minutes. Remove from the pan and top with the feta immediately.

CHAPTER 2

What's for Dinner Tonight?

At my house growing up, dinner had to be "a meal": protein, veggie, and most likely a starch—all pretty much on one plate. There may have been a salad on the side, but otherwise it was like a blue plate special—the kind I used to make fun of as a kid. Now, I completely get the appeal, and I crave that balance. I understand my mom's comment that "it wasn't really a meal" when we'd go to a party with a loaded buffet table. My entire family gets this. Even my teen daughter would come home from high school saying "I haven't had anything to eat all day" when she had an iced latte, a croissant, and a slice of pizza at school. What she's really saying is "I haven't had a real meal"—one that has fed her soul as well as her stomach.

The recipes in this chapter are the answers my family is most likely to hear when it's 5 p.m. and they ask, "What's for dinner?" noticing I haven't even begun to cook. No worries—these "real meals" are designed to be made start to finish in under an hour with minimal cleanup. Some get a head start early in the day with the help of my slow cooker. And some—such as those involving taco filling or meatballs—have the added advantage of freezing well, reducing prep time to minutes. Only the simplest of sides, if any, are needed to round out the meal.

Crunchy Garlic Butter Chicken Cutlets

SERVES 4

If food could turn up in our DNA, cheeseburgers and fried chicken would most certainly be in mine! When I was growing up, my dad had a chain of restaurants called The White Grill, which was famous for both. But I'm not talking just any fried chicken—this was the famous KFC chicken with eleven herbs and spices. Before Colonel Sanders went nationwide with his own chicken chain, he licensed his top secret recipe to a select few outside of Kentucky, and my dad was one of the first. My mom says the deal with the Colonel was simple: Five cents went to Sanders for every chicken dinner sold. The White Grill became so well known for their chicken dinners that my birth announcement in the local newspaper even mentioned that the restaurants would be open and serving chicken on Sunday despite my arrival. My longing for a healthier version of the fried chicken of my youth led me to this recipe. Although it's not the same, it's a fantastic healthy stand-in I make all the time!

CHICKEN

- Avocado oil spray or other nonstick cooking spray, for greasing
- ½ cup all-purpose flour
- 1½ teaspoons Magic Seasoning (page 28)
- 2 large eggs
- ½ cup Italian seasoned breadcrumbs
- ½ cup panko or plain breadcrumbs
- ⅓ cup finely chopped nuts (walnuts, pecans, or almonds)
- 1 pound chicken breast cutlets or 2 chicken breasts, halved horizontally to make 2 thinner pieces

GARLIC BUTTER

- 4 tablespoons (½ stick) butter
- 2 teaspoons minced garlic

1. Preheat the oven to 425°F. Line a baking sheet with parchment paper and spray with avocado oil. Set out three shallow bowls.
2. **MAKE THE CHICKEN:** Mix the flour and Magic Seasoning in the first bowl. Beat the eggs with a fork in the second bowl. Mix the seasoned breadcrumbs, panko, and nuts together in the third bowl.
3. Dip a chicken cutlet (on both sides) first in the seasoned flour, then in the beaten eggs, and lastly in the crumbs, and set on the parchment-lined baking sheet. Repeat with the remaining cutlets and bake for 12 to 15 minutes, until an instant-read thermometer inserted in the center registers 165°F.
4. **MAKE THE GARLIC BUTTER:** Just before serving, melt the butter in a large, wide skillet over medium heat. Add the garlic and sauté for about 30 seconds, or just until golden. Add the baked cutlets to the skillet and let each side brown a little, 1 or 2 minutes.

Man-Pleasing Chicken

SERVES 4

Ridiculous name, incredible dish! No one really knows where this little gem came from, but it's a goodie. Indeed, this is one of my most requested recipes and gets five-star reviews across the board from people of all ages and genders. At this point, we should rename it People-Pleasing Chicken! Hands down, this is the most universal, user-friendly recipe out there. My all-beige eater requests it weekly! And while I think this would be incredible with sautéed mushrooms added to it, my husband, Scooter (who claims to be allergic to mushrooms), wouldn't trust me again if I snuck them in. If you're cooking for your boyfriend for the first time, having company over, or just need a quick dinner that feels fancy, this is it. Serve with roasted broccoli and baked sweet potatoes.

- ½ cup Dijon mustard
- ¼ cup maple syrup
- 1 tablespoon rice wine vinegar
- 4 large or 8 small chicken thighs (any kind will work; I use organic bone-in, skin-on)
- Magic Seasoning (page 28)

1. Preheat the oven to 450°F. Line a large glass baking pan with parchment paper.
2. Mix the mustard, maple syrup, and vinegar in a small bowl.
3. Place the chicken thighs in the baking pan and sprinkle lightly with Magic Seasoning. Pour the sauce over the chicken thighs, turning them to coat. Set them skin-side up.
4. Bake for 40 minutes (rotating the pan 180 degrees halfway through), or until an instant-read thermometer reads 160°F to 165°F when inserted in the thickest part of a thigh, or until juices run clear when cut into with a sharp knife.
5. Remove from the oven and let the chicken rest for 5 minutes before serving.
6. Divide the chicken among plates and spoon some sauce over the top.

Bundt Pan Chicken and Vegetable Dinner

SERVES 4

You can't beat the convenience of rotisserie chicken from the grocery store, but trust me—you can achieve that same crispy-all-over effect by perching your bird on top of the center hole of a Bundt pan (or other large tube pan) before popping it in the oven! Fill the bottom with your favorite combo of hearty vegetables, toss in a few lemon slices and herb sprigs if you so desire, and allow the drippings from the chicken to flavor everything while it roasts. Cleanup couldn't be easier!

- Butter or nonstick cooking spray, for greasing
- One 2½- to 3-pound whole chicken, neck and giblets removed
- 4 tablespoons (½ stick) softened butter
- Salt and pepper
- 1 to 1½ pounds potatoes, cut into 1-inch cubes (3 to 5 cups)
- 12 baby carrots or 1 cup chopped carrots
- 1 small onion, roughly chopped
- 10 garlic cloves, peeled
- 1 to 2 tablespoons avocado oil
- 1 lemon, sliced
- 3 or 4 fresh thyme or rosemary sprigs or 1 teaspoon dried

1. Set a rack on the bottom shelf of the oven and remove the top rack. Preheat the oven to 425°F. Grease the inside of a 10- to 12-cup Bundt pan or tube pan with butter. Cover the center hole of the pan with a piece of foil.
2. Pat the chicken dry with paper towels. Rub the softened butter all over the exterior of the chicken and under the breast skin. Season generously inside and out with salt and pepper.
3. Dump the potatoes, carrots, onion, and garlic into the Bundt pan, drizzle with oil, and season with salt and pepper. Lay the lemon slices and herb sprigs on top.
4. Set the body cavity of the chicken over the foil-covered hole so the neck is pointed upward. Bake for 1 hour, or until an instant-read thermometer reads 165°F when inserted in the breast near the leg/thigh area, or until juices run clear when cut with a sharp knife.
5. To serve, transfer the chicken to a serving platter and carve. With a slotted spoon, transfer the vegetables to a serving bowl, or arrange on the platter around the chicken. Drizzle the pan sauce over everything and serve.

Doritos Chicken

SERVES 4

If ever there was an intersection of Kansas and California, this is it! You get the fried chicken feel, but this chicken is baked. The toughest part is getting the chips turned into crumbs before the kids eat them! Kid 3 is convinced this recipe needs to be made with Cool Ranch Doritos, but I've made it with organic Doritos—yep, those are a thing—and he doesn't even notice. I just need to make sure I hide the bag before he sees it. And you don't have to use Doritos—any chip will work here, although I'd suggest something corn-based or a good corn substitute like Siete chips. You can also swap out the mayo for another creamy sauce, such as ranch dressing or yogurt.

- ¾ cup mayonnaise
- 3 or 4 drops Tabasco or other hot sauce, optional
- 1 to 1½ pounds chicken tenders, tendons removed if desired (see Hack: Easy Chicken Tendon Removal)
- One 9- to 11-ounce bag Doritos or chips of choice (about 2 cups crumbs; see Hack: Leftover Chips and Crackers)
- Nonstick cooking spray
- Magic Seasoning (page 28)

1. Preheat the oven to 375°F. Line a baking sheet with parchment paper. Combine the mayonnaise with the hot sauce, if using, in a large bowl. Add the chicken tenders and stir to coat.
2. Place the Doritos in a food processor and pulse to make coarse crumbs. (Or place the chips in a zip-top bag and crush with a rolling pin.) Place the crumbs in a medium bowl, add the coated chicken tenders, and toss to coat completely.
3. Spray the chicken pieces with cooking spray, sprinkle lightly with the Magic Seasoning, and place on the baking sheet. Bake for 15 to 25 minutes (depending on the size of the tenders), until the chicken is cooked through.

Doritos Fish Tacos

Swap out the mayonnaise with plain yogurt mixed with 1 tablespoon taco seasoning. Instead of chicken tenders, use 1 to 1½ pounds finger-size fish strips cut from halibut or other white fish. Cover the fish with the Dorito crumbs, coat with cooking spray, and place on a parchment-lined baking sheet. Bake in a preheated 425°F oven for 10 minutes on one side, flip, and bake for 5 to 10 minutes longer, until the fish is cooked through. Serve in soft or hard corn or flour tortillas filled with shredded cabbage, guacamole (see Hack: The Best Way to Peel an Avocado and Turn It Into Guacamole, page 102), and mango salsa, with lime wedges for serving.

HACK: Leftover Chips and Crackers

How many half-eaten bags of chips and crackers are in your pantry? I'm embarrassed to tell you how many my kids stuff in mine! Instead of tossing them, I turn them into little baggies of seasoning goodness so I can mix and match different chip/cracker flavors with chicken, fish, or pork; I even add them to meatloaf instead of breadcrumbs! Store them in the freezer for up to 3 months until ready to use.

HACK: Easy Chicken Tendon Removal

Chicken tenders are indeed tender, just as their name implies—except for that annoying tendon, the tough white strand running down the length of each tender that has a texture like a rubber band. Here's a quick and easy way to remove them: A small pair of needle-nose pliers is key. Place a tender on a cutting board with the tendon facing toward you. Locate the tendon with your fingers, place it between the tines of a fork, and press down firmly. With your other hand, grip the end of the tendon with the pliers and pull it free.

Easy, Cheesy Baked Spaghetti and Meatballs

SERVES 4 TO 6

One-pan wonder alert! This is one of those hard-to-believe-it-works dishes, and it's so good! It doesn't taste like you've skipped all the boiling, draining, or making a separate sauce. You literally dump the uncooked pasta, sauce, and water in a 9 x 13-inch baking pan and top with frozen meatballs. Bake in the oven and sprinkle with cheese halfway through—as much or as little as you like.

- 8 to 12 ounces spaghetti or pasta of choice, broken in half
- One 24-ounce jar pasta sauce
- One 18-ounce bag frozen meatballs
- Magic Seasoning (page 28)
- 1½ to 2 cups grated mozzarella-Parmesan cheese blend or an 8-ounce package of drained mini mozzarella balls and 1 cup grated Parmesan
- Fresh basil leaves, optional

1. Preheat the oven to 425°F. Place the uncooked pasta in a 9 x 13-inch baking pan. Pour the sauce over the pasta.
2. Fill the sauce jar with water and pour the water into the baking pan. Give it a few stirs to coat the pasta evenly. Place the frozen meatballs on top. Generously sprinkle with Magic Seasoning.
3. Cover the pan tightly with parchment and then foil, and bake for 30 minutes.
4. Uncover, sprinkle evenly with cheese, and bake uncovered for 15 to 20 minutes more, until the noodles are fully cooked and the cheese is melted. If they still aren't cooked, add about ½ cup water and return to the oven for 5 to 10 minutes. Remove from the oven and top with fresh basil, if using.

Storage Tip

Wrap this casserole tightly with plastic wrap and then foil and refrigerate for up to 4 days, or freeze for up to 3 months.

A Note About Foil

When heating food, I always cover it with a layer of parchment paper before covering with foil to reduce contact with aluminum for health reasons and to help prevent sticking to make cleanup easier. This additional layer also helps to seal in moisture and avoid reactions with acidic foods like tomato sauce that can cause dark spots and leave a "tinny" taste.

Chicken Cordon Bleu Meatballs
with Lemony Dijon Sauce

SERVES 4 TO 6

Kid 2 could live on chicken. She loves it in all forms, but especially in these meatballs. It meets her "beige food preferred" taste buds but delivers for the rest of us, who actually like variety. I love that I can keep extras on hand in the freezer to bake off in the air fryer for an almost-instant main dish. The sauce is amazing on the meatballs but also poured over rice, riced cauliflower, or potatoes. For a lighter take, I'll sometimes skip the cream and just drizzle the hot broth flavored with lemon and mustard over everything.

MEATBALLS

1 pound ground chicken

One 6-ounce package sliced ham, diced

1 small onion, finely chopped

¾ cup grated Swiss cheese

1 large egg, well beaten

2 teaspoons minced garlic

2 teaspoons Magic Seasoning (page 28)

SAUCE

¾ cup low-sodium chicken broth

¼ cup Dijon mustard

1 tablespoon lemon juice, or more, to taste

⅓ cup heavy cream, optional

Salt and pepper, to taste

FOR SERVING

Cooked rice, riced cauliflower, or mashed potatoes

Salad or green vegetable of choice

1. **MAKE THE MEATBALLS:** Preheat the air fryer to 390°F. (Or line a baking sheet with parchment paper and preheat the oven to 350°F.)
2. Mix the chicken, ham, onion, cheese, egg, garlic, and Magic Seasoning in a large bowl. Pinch off bits of the meat mixture and roll into 1½- to 2-inch balls.
3. Place the meatballs in a single layer in the air fryer basket, bake for 8 minutes, give it a shake, and continue cooking for a few minutes longer, until browned and cooked through. (Or place the meatballs on the prepared baking sheet and bake in the preheated oven for about 20 minutes, or until cooked through.)
4. **MAKE THE SAUCE:** Whisk together the broth, mustard, and lemon juice in a small saucepan over high heat and bring it to a boil. Cook for about 5 minutes, or until slightly reduced. Turn the heat to low, stir in the cream, if using, and cook for another minute or two to heat through. Season to taste with salt, pepper, and more lemon juice if you like.
5. **TO SERVE:** Serve the meatballs with rice, riced cauliflower, or potatoes and pour the sauce over top. Add a salad or your favorite green vegetable on the side.

Storage Tip

Put the cooked or uncooked meatballs in a single layer on a parchment-lined baking sheet and place in the freezer until frozen solid, 2 to 4 hours, and then transfer to a freezer bag. Label with the date and use within 2 months. Frozen meatballs—fully cooked or raw—can be reheated or fully cooked without thawing first. If raw, cook for 10 to 12 minutes in the air fryer at 390°F or 25 to 30 minutes in the oven at 350°F. If fully cooked, cook for 6 to 8 minutes in the air fryer or 15 to 20 minutes in the oven.

Winco
STAINLESS
FST-6
#249

Roasted Cod
with Lemon Butter and Capers

SERVES 4

For a very mild, delicate fish like cod, I like to cook it at a higher temp and top it with a buttery sauce before roasting. This helps the exterior caramelize a bit while keeping the interior moist. Elevate the butter sauce with garlic, lemon juice, and pops of briny capers. Bake the fish on a bed of lemon slices to infuse it with bright, citrusy flavor throughout.

- Four 5- to 6-ounce cod fillets
- 1 lemon, thinly sliced
- 2 tablespoons unsalted butter
- Juice of 1 lemon
- 2 tablespoons capers, drained
- 2 teaspoons chopped garlic
- 1 teaspoon Magic Seasoning (page 28)

1. Pat the fish dry with paper towels.
2. Set a rack in the middle of the oven and preheat the oven to 425°F. Line a large, rimmed baking sheet with parchment paper and set the fish fillets on top, tucking lemon slices under each.
3. Place the butter in a microwave-safe measuring cup or bowl and melt in the microwave. Add the lemon juice, capers, garlic, and Magic Seasoning and whisk to combine.
4. Pour the sauce evenly over the fillets and roast in the oven for 9 to 12 minutes. To test for doneness, press the top gently with your fork or your finger to see if the flesh flakes, or insert a thin-bladed knife in the center and see if it feels warm when pressed against your wrist.

Pesto-Glazed Salmon
with Roasted Asparagus and Cherry Tomatoes

SERVES 4

Some types of fish—especially thick, oily, delicate ones such as salmon—lend themselves well to low, slow cooking, which ensures that they cook evenly and the results are melt-in-your-mouth tender and juicy. Another benefit to this method: Your kitchen won't smell fishy for hours afterward! A tender veggie such as asparagus or cherry tomatoes (or both!) can roast on the same pan right alongside the salmon for a full meal.

- Four 5- to 6-ounce salmon fillets, skin-on or skinless
- One 12- to 16-ounce bunch medium-size fresh asparagus, trimmed of woody stems
- 1 to 2 cups halved cherry tomatoes or grape tomatoes
- 1 tablespoon olive oil or avocado oil
- Pinch or two of Magic Seasoning (page 28) or salt and pepper
- 2 tablespoons grated Parmesan, optional
- ¼ to ½ cup prepared pesto
- Lemon wedges, for serving

1. Pat the fish dry with paper towels.
2. Set a rack in the middle of the oven and preheat the oven to 275°F. Line a large, rimmed baking sheet with parchment paper.
3. Place the asparagus and tomatoes on the baking sheet and toss with the oil and Magic Seasoning. Allow the veggies to take up half of the baking sheet, leaving the other half empty. Sprinkle with the Parmesan, if using.
4. Roast for 5 minutes if the asparagus is thin or 10 minutes if it's thicker. Remove the baking sheet from the oven and add the salmon to the empty side. Sprinkle lightly with the Magic Seasoning, and top each fillet with 1 or 2 tablespoons pesto.
5. Return the baking sheet to the oven and roast for 20 to 30 minutes or longer, depending on how thick the fillets are and how well done you like your salmon. To test for doneness, press the top gently with your fork or your finger to see if the flesh flakes, or insert a thin-bladed knife in the center and see if it feels warm when pressed against your wrist.

Tip

If the asparagus is still a little too hard for your taste, remove the salmon fillets and pop the pan back in the oven for another 5 minutes or so.

Turkey Salisbury Steaks
with Red Onion Gravy

SERVES 4

I'm pretty sure my introduction to Salisbury steak was either a Swanson frozen dinner—remember the one with the corn and a brownie for dessert?—or the school cafeteria. Honestly, both were a little dreadful, right? Luckily, these aren't! They are so good and one of Scooter's and picky Kid 2's favorites! Oh, and don't be afraid to make the gravy. It's easy, it's magical, and it's going to make you feel like a fancy chef!

- 1 pound ground turkey
- 1 large red onion, half diced, half thinly sliced, divided
- 1 large egg
- 1 tablespoon Worcestershire sauce
- 2 teaspoons Magic Seasoning (page 28), divided
- 1 cup all-purpose flour, divided, plus more if needed
- 2 to 4 tablespoons avocado oil, for frying
- 2 to 3 cups cold water or chicken broth

FOR SERVING

- Mashed potatoes or cooked rice
- Cooked green vegetable or salad of choice

1. Place the turkey, diced onion, egg, Worcestershire sauce, and 1 teaspoon Magic Seasoning in a large bowl and combine well with your hands.
2. Divide the mixture into four portions and form into patties. Place ¾ cup flour on a plate. Set another paper towel–lined plate beside the stove.
3. Heat 2 tablespoons oil in a 12-inch heavy skillet with a lid over medium heat. Dredge each patty in the flour on both sides, place in the skillet, and fry, turning gently once, taking care to stop it from falling apart (a fish spatula works well for this), until browned on both sides, about 2 minutes per side. Remove to the paper towel–lined plate. (Do this in batches, if necessary.)
4. Add 1 or 2 more tablespoons oil, depending on how much fat is left in the skillet. Add the sliced onions and sauté until lightly browned and tender, about 5 minutes.
5. Combine the remaining ¼ cup flour and 1 teaspoon Magic Seasoning with 2 cups of water in a large measuring cup, whisk until smooth, and then add to the pan. Cook, stirring until thickened, 1 or 2 minutes. Add a little more liquid if it seems too thick.
6. Return the patties to the pan. Reduce the heat to a gentle simmer, cover with a lid, and cook for about 15 minutes, or until the turkey is cooked through.
7. Serve the patties on plates with the gravy on top, along with mashed potatoes or rice and your favorite green vegetable or a salad.

Skillet-Roasted Lemon and Maple Chicken Thighs

SERVES 4

This chicken is so flavorful, it's hard to believe you need only five ingredients, one pan, and barely half an hour, if that, in the kitchen! When halved lemons and skin-on chicken pieces are left to caramelize together, something truly magical happens. A drizzle of sweetness is all that's needed to take it over the top! The pan juices would also be wonderful drizzled over rice or whatever veggie you choose.

4 large bone-in, skin-on chicken thighs

Magic Seasoning (page 28) or salt and pepper

1 tablespoon avocado oil

2 lemons, halved

2 to 3 tablespoons maple syrup

Fresh thyme sprigs, for serving, optional

1. Remove the top rack of the oven, if necessary, to accommodate a large skillet. Preheat the oven to 450°F.
2. Pat the chicken thighs dry with paper towels and season lightly all over with Magic Seasoning.
3. Place a heavy oven-safe skillet large enough to accommodate the chicken and lemon halves over medium heat, add the oil, and swirl to coat.
4. Arrange the chicken thighs skin-side down in the skillet and wedge the lemon halves, cut-side down, in between them. Let cook, undisturbed, until the chicken skin becomes crispy and caramelized and the lemons begin to char, about 12 minutes.
5. Use tongs to carefully lift the lemons out onto a plate and brush the cut sides with the maple syrup. Return the lemons to the pan, cut-side down. Place the pan in the oven for 5 minutes.
6. Remove the pan from the oven and flip the chicken thighs over, skin-side up, leaving the lemons cut-side down. Brush the tops of the chicken thighs with a little maple syrup, if desired.
7. Return the pan to the oven for 5 more minutes, or until the top of the chicken becomes crispy and deeply caramelized and an instant-read thermometer reaches 165°F to 175°F when inserted into the thickest part of a thigh. (Or check for doneness by cutting into a thigh and seeing if the juices run clear.)
8. Transfer the thighs with tongs to a platter or serving plates, squeeze the lemons over them, and spoon some of the pan juices over each serving. Top with fresh thyme, if desired.

HACK: The Fastest and Easiest Way to Tackle Caked-On Grime on Pots and Pans

Set a dishwashing pod in the pan and pour boiling water over it. Let it sit for about 30 minutes. Scrub with a sponge or scrubbing pad, and your pan should look good as new! You can also set a couple of tablespoons of baking soda in the pan and cover with equal parts boiling water and vinegar.

In-N-Out Animal-Style Burgers

MAKES 4 "DOUBLE DOUBLE" BURGERS

In-N-Out is famous for their "double double" cheeseburger made with two extra-thin patties, which Scooter and Kid 3 always order (Kid 2 and I do a single). And this is important: We all order ours "Animal Style"—a not-so-secret off-menu item that has a cult following. The mustard is added to the grill before the patty goes down, so the tangy flavor bakes into the meat. The patties are sandwiched with grilled onions, dill pickle slices, and extra special sauce along with the usual "hand-leafed" lettuce and tomato. We are such huge fans of the burger that's synonymous with Los Angeles that I came up with my own interpretation at home, along with all the extras that make them so special.

- 2 pounds ground beef
- 4 soft hamburger buns
- Avocado oil spray or other nonstick cooking spray, for greasing
- Magic Seasoning (page 28) or salt and pepper
- About 8 teaspoons yellow mustard (preferably from a squeeze bottle)
- 8 slices American cheese
- ½ batch Skillet-Grilled Onions (page 85)
- About ½ cup Animal-Style Burger Sauce (page 85)
- 1 large tomato, sliced
- Iceberg lettuce leaves
- Dill pickle slices, optional

1. Line two large baking sheets with parchment paper. Form the beef into eight patties, place them on one of the baking sheets, and flatten them as thinly as possible with a spatula. If you're cooking the burgers in batches, preheat the oven to 200°F.
2. Heat a large skillet, griddle, or outdoor flat-top grill to medium heat and toast the buns, cut-side down, until golden brown and crispy, 3 or 4 minutes. Transfer to a platter.
3. Wipe any crumbs off the skillet surface and spray with avocado oil. Increase the heat to medium-high (about 460°F on an electric griddle). Season the skillet with Magic Seasoning. (This ensures that the burgers will be seasoned more evenly from the start.)
4. Squirt about a teaspoon of mustard directly onto the skillet and then place a patty on top. Repeat with the remaining patties and sprinkle the tops lightly with more Magic Seasoning. (You may need to do this in batches.) Cook until crispy and browned, about 2 minutes, and then flip and cook 1 or 2 minutes longer. Top each with a slice of cheese.
5. Transfer the cooked patties to the other parchment-lined baking sheet. If cooking in batches, place the patties in a baking pan at least 2 inches deep and cover the pan with foil, making sure the foil doesn't touch the cheese. Place the pan in the warm oven while you repeat with the remaining patties and cheese slices. When all are cooked, add mounds of grilled onions to four of the patties. Stack the onion-topped patties on the cheese-only patties.
6. Spread the bottom buns generously with the Animal-Style Sauce, top each with a tomato slice, sprinkle with a little Magic Seasoning, and add a few lettuce leaves.
7. Use a spatula to place each burger stack on top of the lettuce. Add a few dill pickle slices and more Animal Sauce, if desired. Add the top bun and serve immediately.

Tip

Have the sauce, sides, buns, and toppings ready before you start making the burgers; they cook up super-fast. An outdoor flat-top grill (we use a Blackstone) or large electric griddle is ideal for cooking all the patties at once. A large, heavy skillet or griddle on top of the stove will do the trick as well if you work quickly.

Animal-Style Tots

SERVES 8

In-N-Out's Animal-Style Fries are almost as famous as their burgers. For my home version, I substitute tater tots baked on a baking sheet for the fries. This recipe supposedly serves eight, but our family of four can always ensure that no tot goes to waste.

One 32-ounce bag frozen tater tots (not pre-seasoned)

Magic Seasoning (page 28)

6 to 8 slices American cheese or about ½ cup store-bought cheddar cheese sauce

½ batch Skillet-Grilled Onions (page 85)

½ cup Animal-Style Burger Sauce (page 85)

1. Preheat the oven to 400°F. Line a baking sheet with parchment paper. (Or follow the instructions on your bag of tater tots.)
2. Spread out the tater tots on the parchment and sprinkle lightly with Magic Seasoning. Toss to coat and bake according to the package directions.
3. Remove the tots from the oven, lay the cheese slices over top to cover, and then return them to the oven for about 1 minute, just long enough for the cheese to melt.
4. Transfer the tots to a serving bowl or platter. Top with the grilled onions and Animal-Style Sauce.

Tip

The tots will also cook up nice and crispy in an air fryer set at 400°F in half the time. Place about half the bag of tots in a single layer in the air fryer basket, season lightly with Magic Seasoning, air-fry for 6 minutes, shake the basket to toss, and then air-fry for another 4 or 5 minutes, until golden brown and crispy.

Animal-Style Burger Sauce

MAKES ABOUT 1⅓ CUPS

The formula for In-N-Out's famous sauce is supposedly top secret, but multitudes claim to have cracked it. Most versions are basically varying proportions of mayo, ketchup, and relish with a splash of this or that. Here's how I make it! To make this low-carb, use unsweetened ketchup, dill or no-sugar-added pickle relish, and a few drops of liquid stevia or monk fruit. This makes enough for four hefty "double doubles" (see In-N-Out Animal-Style Burgers, page 81) plus a batch of Animal-Style Tots (page 82), and maybe a little extra for a sandwich later in the week.

- ¾ cup mayonnaise
- 6 tablespoons ketchup
- ¼ cup sweet pickle relish
- Few drops Worcestershire sauce

1. Mix the mayonnaise, ketchup, relish, and Worcestershire sauce together in a small bowl. Cover and refrigerate for up to 5 days.

Skillet-Grilled Onions

MAKES ABOUT 1 CUP

These onions work on so many things! Honestly, I'm excited when we have some left over! They're amazing on sausages for dinner or in an omelet or scramble for breakfast. Toss them inside a panini and take your sandwich to the next level!

- 2 tablespoons avocado oil
- 2 large yellow or red onions, halved and thinly sliced
- Magic Seasoning (page 28)
- 1 garlic clove, minced
- ½ teaspoon balsamic vinegar
- ½ teaspoon Worcestershire sauce

1. Heat the oil in a large skillet over medium heat. Add the onions, season lightly with Magic Seasoning, and cook, stirring occasionally, until softened, about 5 minutes.
2. Add the garlic, vinegar, and Worcestershire sauce and continue cooking until deep golden brown and crispy, 3 to 5 minutes longer.

HACK: Meat Grease Disposal

How do you strain the grease off your cooked meat without clogging up your drain? Place a sheet of foil on the bottom of your sink and press down to form a cup shape inside the drain. Hold a strainer with the cooked meat directly over the "cup" and allow it to catch the grease. Fold up the sides of the foil to form a package and drop it in the trash. You save your drain, and cleanup couldn't be easier! And for the times when there's not a ton of grease, grab a paper towel and use tongs to soak up the grease directly in the pan. Then drop the greasy towel into the garbage.

Baked Cheeseburgers

SERVES 4

When it comes to burgers, there's either thick or thin . . . no in-between. We are a thin burger family, and specifically, we eat flat-top burgers—cooked on a griddle over onions and flattened with a spatula so that the onions steam and permeate the patties as they cook. Here's why: In the 1920s, when my dad was in his teens, his first job was at a White Castle. That job sparked his desire to open his own restaurants, which were fittingly called The White Grill. I do a similar version, but instead of cooking it on a flat top, I put mine in the oven. I don't make patties, either; I just plop the whole chunk of beef on top of the onions, spread it to the edges of the pan, and cut it into squares—the shape of the fast-food burgers of my childhood! This is a favorite in my house of picky eaters—no greasy mess, and cleanup is a breeze! To keep this low-carb, I eat mine on sliced keto bread, but Scooter and the kids have theirs on buns. (If you want to get fancy, ciabatta rolls will fit the square shape nicely.)

- 1 medium onion, thinly sliced
- 1 teaspoon Magic Seasoning (page 28), divided
- 1 pound lean ground beef
- Four 1-ounce cheese slices (such as American, cheddar, or Monterey Jack)
- 4 hamburger buns or ciabatta rolls
- Condiments and toppings of choice

1. Preheat the oven to 400°F.
2. Place the onions evenly on the bottom of an 8- or 9-inch square baking pan and season them with ½ teaspoon Magic Seasoning. Dump the ground beef on top, pressing evenly with a spatula or your hands to the edges of the pan. Sprinkle with the remaining seasoning.
3. Bake for 15 minutes, or until the meat is no longer pink. Top with the cheese and return to the oven for a few more minutes, until the cheese is melted.
4. To serve, cut into squares with a spatula and serve naked or in a bun with your favorite accompaniments.

French Onion Soup Burgers

Place the meat in a medium bowl and season with a 2-ounce package of dry onion soup (such as Knorr). Mix with your hands and then dump the meat into the baking pan. Proceed with step 3, and top with Swiss or Gruyère cheese.

Taco Burgers

Place the meat in a medium bowl and season with 1 tablespoon taco seasoning. Mix with your hands and then dump the meat into the baking pan. Proceed with step 3, and top with sliced Pepper Jack or shredded Mexican cheese blend.

Greek Burgers

Place the meat in a medium bowl and season with 1½ teaspoons dried oregano or 1 tablespoon Greek seasoning blend. Mix with your hands and then dump the meat into the baking pan. Proceed with step 3, and top with 1 cup crumbled feta.

Pizza Burgers

Place the meat in a medium bowl and season with 1½ teaspoons dried oregano or 1 tablespoon Italian seasoning. Mix with your hands and then dump the meat into the baking pan. Proceed with step 3, and top with sliced mozzarella or shredded Italian cheese blend.

Lizzie's Classic Sloppy Joes

MAKES 4

Sloppy joes tend to bring to mind school cafeterias and lunch ladies, but those of us from the Midwest take our sloppy joes a bit more seriously. While some say they were invented in Key West at the famous bar of the same name, the other theory—and the one I'm sticking to—is that they were created by a cook named Joe at a diner in Sioux City, Iowa, during the Great Depression. Back then it was called a "loose meat sandwich" and consisted of little more than beef, onions, and mustard. But over time, the recipe evolved, and it soon became a school cafeteria fixture all over the country. Homemade sloppy joes are still a hit at my house with kids and grown-ups alike. I generally go by my late friend Lizzie's formula, which has the perfect balance of sweet, tang, and gentle spice. While she's no longer with us, her spirit lives on in her Kansas version. To fully appreciate sloppy joes in all of their messy glory, be sure to serve them on your favorite buns with a jumbo roll of paper towels and potato chips for scooping up the spillage.

- 1 pound ground beef or other meat or meat alternative
- ½ large onion, chopped
- 1 cup ketchup
- 1 tablespoon lemon juice
- 1 tablespoon white vinegar
- 1 tablespoon Worcestershire sauce
- 1 teaspoon brown sugar
- 1 teaspoon paprika
- ½ teaspoon dry mustard
- Salt and pepper, to taste
- 4 soft hamburger buns, split

1. Place the ground beef and onion in a large nonstick skillet and cook over medium-high heat until the meat is browned and onion is soft, 8 to 10 minutes.
2. Add the ketchup, lemon juice, vinegar, Worcestershire sauce, brown sugar, paprika, and mustard. Reduce the heat to low, cover, and cook for about 30 minutes, stirring occasionally, until the flavors meld. Season to taste with salt and pepper.
3. Serve on hamburger buns.

Large-Batch Sloppy Joes

To make a large batch, double or triple the ingredients and place in a slow cooker, give it a good stir, and cook on low for 4 to 6 hours, until the flavors have melded. Uncover, stir again to break up the meat, and serve on hamburger buns.

Storage Tip

To freeze and reheat, cool the meat mixture completely, place in freezer-safe containers or bags, and freeze for up to 6 months. Thaw in the fridge overnight before reheating in the microwave or a skillet over medium heat, adding a splash of water if necessary.

Pulled BBQ Chicken Sandwiches

MAKES 8

Having grown up so close to one of the country's major barbecue meccas, I have strong opinions about the style of sauce I prefer: thick, brick-red, and caramel-sweet with just the right balance of tang and spice. There are so many great brands at the grocery store these days, so there's no need to stress trying to recreate it. In this recipe, I use a whole bottle to recreate my own healthier version of Kansas City–style barbecue sandwiches at home, using pulled chicken instead of firing up the grill. This recipe basically makes itself, and to make it even easier, be sure to try my hack for "pulling" the tender meat into bite-size shreds right in the pot you cooked it in!

- 1½ pounds boneless, skinless chicken breasts
- 1½ pounds boneless, skinless chicken thighs
- One 18-ounce bottle Kansas City–style barbecue sauce
- 8 hamburger buns
- Creamy and Tangy Coleslaw (page 123)
- Yellow mustard, optional
- Dill pickle slices, optional

1. Place the chicken breasts and thighs in a 5- to 6-quart slow cooker and cover with the barbecue sauce, turning with a wooden spoon to coat all the pieces.
2. Cover with the lid and cook on low for 6 to 7 hours or on high for 2 to 3 hours, until the chicken is tender enough to shred.
3. Transfer the pieces to a cutting board or pan and shred with 2 forks (or try my faster Hack: Shredded Chicken).
4. Return the shredded chicken to the slow cooker (if you removed it) and stir with the sauce.
5. Toast the buns, if desired, pile with the chicken, and top with slaw. Add mustard and pickle slices if you like.

HACK: Shredded Chicken

To shred the chicken, leave the chicken in the slow cooker, turn off the heat, and shred with a pastry blender.

HACK: Rotisserie Chicken Shortcut

Don't have hours to wait on a slow cooker? Grab a rotisserie chicken instead, shred it up (see Hack: Debone a Rotisserie Chicken in Two Minutes, page 106), mix it up in a large nonstick skillet with the barbecue sauce, and let it simmer on medium-low heat just until heated through, 10 to 15 minutes.

Weeknight Croque Monsieurs

SERVES 4

I know what you're thinking: What's a fancy French sandwich doing in a book like this? Well, here's the thing. I fell in love with this sandwich on my first trip to France. And since mastering the art of saying "jambon et fromage" was way easier than figuring out how to say "please, no snails," I ate a ton of 'em! I truly thought there was some mysterious preparation that made these out of reach for those of us who hadn't attended Le Cordon Bleu. But basically, it's just a very affordable way of rejiggering a ham and cheese sandwich. Go as highbrow or as lowbrow as you wish on the cheese. Gruyère is traditional, but good old Swiss will do the trick just fine. And don't skimp on the creamy, buttery bechamel sauce, which is key.

- 8 slices bread, any kind (I've even used a hot dog bun turned inside out)
- 2 tablespoons butter
- 2 tablespoons all-purpose flour
- 1½ cups milk
- Salt and pepper, to taste
- Pinch of ground nutmeg, optional
- 2 or 3 tablespoons Dijon mustard, optional
- 8 slices (about 5 ounces) deli ham or turkey
- 8 slices Gruyère, Swiss, or mild cheddar cheese
- Grated pecorino Romano or Parmesan

1. Set a rack 5 to 6 inches from the broiler unit and another one in the center of the oven. Line a baking sheet with parchment and arrange the slices of bread in two rows on top. Preheat the oven to 400°F.
2. **MAKE THE BECHAMEL:** Melt the butter in a medium saucepan over medium heat. Add the flour and then cook and stir for 3 minutes, or until well combined.
3. Slowly pour in the milk, whisking constantly, until smooth. Cook and stir until thickened, a few minutes more. Season to taste with the salt, pepper, and nutmeg, if using. (This may be made ahead and refrigerated for up to a week.)
4. Spread the mustard, if using, onto each bread slice. Then spread on a generous amount of bechamel sauce. Top four of the bread slices with two slices of ham each. Then top all eight slices with the cheese. Place the slices without ham on top of the ones with the ham, with the cheese and bechamel side facing up, to make four sandwiches. Top with more bechamel and then sprinkle the tops with pecorino.
5. Place the baking sheet on the center rack of the oven and bake for about 5 minutes, or until the cheese inside the sandwich melts.
6. Switch the oven temperature to broil, move the baking sheet to the upper rack, and broil the sandwiches for 3 or 4 minutes, watching carefully, just until bubbly. Serve hot.

Tip

To make a Thanksgiving Croque Monsieur, substitute turkey for the ham and add a layer of cranberry sauce to the four bread slices meant for the bottom of the sandwich before adding the bechamel, turkey, and cheese.

Panini Reubens

SERVES 4

Growing up, I'd only see corned beef in the Crock-Pot around St. Patrick's Day, and I couldn't stand it. It looked like such a bore, hanging out with boiled potatoes and cooked cabbage! Here's the funny part: I have always loved Reuben sandwiches. Of course, as a kid, I never made the connection. Today I absolutely love corned beef in any form. But I have to admit, the only reason I throw a brisket into the Crock-Pot for St. Paddy's Day nowadays is for the leftovers it generates to make Reubens the next night. They're always a hit with the whole family. My panini press melts the cheese and crisps the bread to perfection, making the process even easier!

- 2 tablespoons softened butter
- 8 slices rye bread (pumpernickel, marble, or sourdough would also be good)
- ¼ to ½ cup Thousand Island dressing, Russian dressing, or Animal-Style Burger Sauce (page 85), or to taste
- One 14.5-ounce can sauerkraut, drained and squeezed dry (about 1 cup)
- ½ pound corned beef, thinly sliced
- 4 to 8 slices Swiss cheese

1. Close the panini press and heat for 5 minutes.
2. Butter one side of each bread slice. Flip over and spread the other side of each slice with the dressing. Top four of the slices with sauerkraut, corned beef, 1 or 2 slices of cheese, and the remaining bread, buttered side up.
3. Place the sandwiches on the hot panini press. Close the lid and grill for 5 minutes, or until the cheese is melted and grill marks appear. Serve hot.

Tip

No panini press? No problem! You can also do this in a skillet or on a griddle. Toast the sandwiches on one side over medium-low heat as you would a grilled cheese and then flip and press them down with a heavy lid or the bottom of a small skillet until crispy on both sides. Alternatively, cook them one at a time in your waffle iron for more crispy edges!

Pesto Pizza

To dress up a basic cheese or pepperoni pizza, pour pesto into a sandwich baggie and snip off the end. Squeeze the bag to pipe the pesto over the top of the warm pizza.

Philly Cheesesteak Pizza

In step 3, spread alfredo sauce onto the crust and then top with sliced leftover steak, provolone cheese, and thinly sliced onions and bell peppers (sautéed first for extra caramelization).

Kansas City BBQ Chicken

In step 3, spread Kansas City–style BBQ sauce onto the crust and then top with BBQ chicken (see Pulled BBQ Chicken Sandwiches, page 90), sliced red onion, shredded mozzarella cheese, and chopped cilantro. Serve with ranch dressing, if desired.

Half-Homemade California Summer Pizza

MAKES ONE 8- TO 12-INCH PIE

While most people think of New York and Chicago when they think of American pizza, I'm here to tell ya, the pizza game in Los Angeles is strong! Here you'll generally find a thinner crust and lighter ingredients because of the year-round produce we're super lucky to have. The crust is more of a vehicle for the star toppings (pun intended). It's amazing what you can use for the pizza crust: canned crescent roll dough, ready-made dough from the deli, gluten-free boxed mixes (such as Simple Mills' almond flour and Bob's Red Mill gluten-free crust mixes), and even riced cauliflower. This recipe makes one medium pie. To feed the whole family, I'll double the ingredients and top another rolled-out crust to have ready to slide into the oven when the other comes out, so everyone can dig into their first slice while it's hot.

All-purpose flour, for dusting

One ½-pound ball pizza dough, room temperature, or dough prepared from a mix

Olive oil, for brushing, optional

2 tablespoons prepared pesto

4 ounces shredded mozzarella or Italian blend cheese

1 cup diced fresh tomatoes, halved cherry tomatoes, or Roasted Cherry Tomatoes (page 127)

½ cup fresh corn kernels, raw or cooked (see Hack)

½ cup ricotta

Drizzle of balsamic glaze

¼ cup fresh torn basil leaves, optional

1. Place a pizza stone on the lowest rack of the oven. (Or make a makeshift pizza stone by flipping over a baking sheet and setting it in the oven.) Preheat the oven to 500°F.
2. Place a piece of parchment paper on a work surface, dust with flour, and set the ball of dough (also dusted with flour) on top. Set another piece of parchment on top of the dough and roll the dough out about ¼ inch thick, no larger than the pizza stone. (This technique works great for gluten-free dough.)
3. Remove the top piece of parchment. Brush the crust with oil with a pastry brush or the back of a spoon, if desired. Spread the pesto in the center, sprinkle with the mozzarella, and then top with the tomatoes and corn. Drop dollops of the ricotta (I use a small ice cream scoop) over the top.
4. Pull out the rack with the heated pizza stone. Holding the sides of the parchment, carefully transfer the crust on the paper to the pizza stone.
5. Bake for 10 to 15 minutes, until the crust is golden and the cheese is bubbly. Slide the pizza on its paper onto a cutting board or serving platter. Drizzle with the balsamic glaze and garnish with basil, if using.

HACK: Shucking and Stripping Corn

The fastest way to cook and shuck fresh corn without turning on the stove, the oven, or the grill is to microwave the ears, in the husk! Choose the freshest-looking ears, with tight, bright green husks and shiny silks. Rinse them off and pop them in the microwave on high for about 2 minutes for one ear, adding a minute or two for each additional ear. Let cool and then cut off the stem ends and slip off the husks and the silks.

For a cleaner, safer way to strip corn, your trusty Bundt pan comes to the rescue! To keep kernels from flying around or cutting yourself as you try to keep the cob from slipping, try this: Insert the tip of the cob into the center hole of your pan so it's held secure in an upright position. Holding the top end, use your other hand to cut the kernels with a sharp knife from top to bottom, allowing the kernels to fall into the pan.

Taco Bell–Style Tacos

MAKES ABOUT 12

I love Taco Bell, and I'm not embarrassed to admit it. My Taco Bell order from my teenage years is still my order today: one Burrito Supreme, no beans or rice, and one Taco Supreme, with two packets of Taco Bell Mild Sauce. I'm not surprised that my kids keep asking for it! So I came up with a healthier version of the meat filling for Taco Tuesdays at home. It's so easy! You can make this in bulk and freeze it, it works with any meat, and it's endlessly customizable. I make this so often that I buy taco seasoning in bulk. And if you find yourself at Taco Bell, save yourself a few pennies by picking up some extra sauce packets!

TACO BELL–STYLE SEASONED MEAT

1 pound lean ground meat (beef, pork, chicken, turkey, or plant-based)

1 small to medium onion, finely chopped

One 1-ounce package taco seasoning

FOR SERVING

12 hard taco shells or soft flour or corn tortillas

Hot sauce or salsa of choice (I use Taco Bell Mild Sauce)

TOPPINGS, OPTIONAL

Black beans

Refried beans

Shredded cheddar or Mexican blend cheese

Pickled jalapeño slices

Shredded lettuce

Diced onions

Diced tomatoes

Guacamole (see Hack: The Best Way to Peel an Avocado and Turn It Into Guacamole, page 102)

Sour cream

1. **MAKE THE TACO MEAT:** Place the meat, onion, and seasoning in a large nonstick skillet. Cook over medium heat, breaking up the meat with a wooden spoon and stirring occasionally, until the onion is tender and the meat is thoroughly cooked, 15 to 20 minutes. If all the liquid evaporates and the seasoning starts to stick to the pan, stir in water, 1 tablespoon at a time, until you get the consistency you're after.
2. **TO SERVE**: Fill each taco shell with about 2 tablespoons of the cooked meat. If using soft tortillas, warm each for a few seconds on each side in a dry skillet over high heat, or by placing three or four at a time on a microwave-safe plate, covering with a slightly damp paper towel, and microwaving on high for about 30 seconds, or until warm.
3. Drizzle with hot sauce or salsa and add toppings of choice.

Large-Batch Taco Meat

Double or triple the amount of meat, onion, and seasoning and place in a slow cooker with ½ cup tomato salsa per pound of meat. Cook on low for 4 to 6 hours, until the flavors meld. Serve or divide among airtight containers and freeze for up to 6 months.

HACK: Extra-Crispy Baked Tacos

Preheat the oven to 350°F. Place hard taco shells in a baking pan, standing them straight up. If there's space in the baking pan, fill it with tortilla chips. Add a layer of grated cheese or nacho cheese into each taco shell. Then add cooked Taco Bell–Style Seasoned Meat and more cheese. Bake for 3 to 5 minutes, just long enough to warm the shells and melt the cheese. (You can also flip a muffin pan upside down and place the shells between the cups.)

Walking Tacos—for 5, 10, or 100!

Tacos are guaranteed crowd-pleasers, but they can devolve into a crumbly mess when plates aren't involved—and maybe not even tables and chairs. Walking tacos are great for the kitchen table or the standing room–only patio! Open individual bags of Fritos *or* Doritos (we only use Doritos, but honestly any tortilla-type chip will work here!) and spoon in warmed Taco Bell–Style Seasoned Taco Meat (see page 98) over the chips. Add desired toppings and serve with a napkin and fork. (And if you don't have the little bags, just put them in individual bowls.)

BAKER'S BEST

Taco Bell–Style Pizza

SERVES 4 TO 6

Here's another fast-food fave that works as an easy home-cooked meal!

8 to 12 five- or six-inch corn tortillas

Nonstick cooking spray

One 16-ounce can refried beans, warmed

1 batch Taco Bell–Style Seasoned Meat (about 3 cups; page 98)

1 to 2 cups shredded Mexican blend cheese, divided

One 15-ounce jar red enchilada sauce

TOPPINGS, OPTIONAL

Sliced black olives

Shredded lettuce

Sour cream

Diced tomatoes

Sliced scallions

1. Preheat the oven to 425°F. Line a baking sheet with parchment paper.
2. Place the tortillas on the baking sheet. Spray the tops with cooking spray and bake for 2 minutes. Spread a thin layer of refried beans on half of the tortillas and top with a layer of the cooked meat, followed by a layer of cheese. Top each pizza with a remaining tortilla.
3. Spoon the enchilada sauce on top, followed by more cheese. Bake for 5 to 10 minutes, until the cheese is melted. Remove from the oven and garnish as desired.

Taco Tuesday Casserole

SERVES 4

Some folks call this tamale pie, but I knew if I did, I'd be running the risk my kids might not try it—although the fact that it's beige did increase the chances Kid 2 would at least give it a whirl. Taco Casserole sounds more approachable when you're dealing with picky eaters. It's fancy enough to serve if you have guests coming over. It helps stretch that taco meat, too.

- Two 8.5-ounce boxes Jiffy Corn Muffin mix
- One 14.75-ounce can creamed corn
- One 15.25-ounce can whole kernel corn, drained
- ⅔ cup milk (any kind)
- 2 large eggs
- 1 batch Taco Bell–Style Seasoned Meat (about 3 cups; page 98)
- One 10-ounce can Ro-Tel Mild Diced Tomatoes and Green Chilies, undrained
- Nonstick cooking spray
- One 8-ounce package Mexican blend shredded cheese

TOPPINGS, OPTIONAL

- Black beans
- Refried beans
- Shredded cheddar or Mexican blend cheese
- Pickled jalapeño slices
- Shredded lettuce
- Diced onions
- Diced tomatoes
- Guacamole (see Hack)
- Sour cream

1. Preheat the oven to 350°F. Mix the muffin mix, creamed corn, whole corn, milk, and eggs in a medium bowl until well combined.
2. Reheat the cooked meat in a large skillet and then add the Ro-Tel, juice and all. Mix well, cover, and simmer until hot, about 5 minutes.
3. Spray the bottom of a 9-inch square baking pan with cooking spray and then pour in half the batter. Add the meat and then cover with the cheese. Top with the remaining batter.
4. Bake for 35 to 40 minutes, until the cornbread is cooked through and a cake tester comes out clean. Serve with your favorite taco toppings.

Storage Tip

Wrap this casserole tightly with plastic wrap and then foil and refrigerate for up to 4 days, or freeze for up to 3 months.

To reheat: If frozen, thaw in the refrigerator overnight. Unwrap and then cover with a layer of parchment and foil to prevent over-browning and place in a 350°F oven for 20 to 30 minutes, long enough to heat through.

HACK: The Best Way to Peel an Avocado and Turn It Into Guacamole

Cut the avocado all the way around the seed lengthwise and then turn and cut it all the way around crosswise through the center to make four sections. Twist it apart and the skin pops right off! To make my guac, I put the peeled avocado in a bowl, season it to taste with Magic Seasoning (page 28) and lime or lemon juice, add chopped onion and tomato if I have it, and mash it up. To keep your guac from turning brown, place it in an airtight storage container and then flatten the top with a spoon to remove any air bubbles. Pour ½ inch of water over the top, cover with a lid or plastic wrap, and pop it in the fridge for up to 3 days. Pour off the water and stir before serving.

Fred & Red's Spaghetti Red Chili

SERVES 8 TO 12

Open since 1923, Fred & Red's Chili in Joplin, Missouri, is one of those places that was old even when I was little . . . like your grandma: She's always the same age no matter what age you are. The dish they are most famous for is "spaghetti red": a huge pile of noodles topped with chili, onions, and pickles and always served with saltines on the side. A lot of folks would call this Cincinnati chili, but Fred & Red's has a taste all its own. The recipe is supposedly top secret, but this one comes pretty close. There are no tomatoes or onions in the meat mixture; it's all about the seasoning (Williams brand) and the crushed crackers that are stirred in to thicken it, creating a smooth chili that's great for topping a cheeseburger or hot dog and, yes, a bowl of spaghetti! Don't try to rush this one; the longer it simmers, the better it gets. The flavor improves even more after a day or two in the fridge, and it freezes great.

- 2 pounds ground beef
- One 1-ounce package Williams Chili Seasoning (or your favorite brand)
- 1 teaspoon ground cumin
- 1 teaspoon crushed garlic
- 1½ teaspoons salt, plus more to taste
- 2½ cups water
- ¾ cup saltine cracker meal (about 20 finely crushed crackers)

FOR SERVING

- Cooked spaghetti noodles
- Shredded cheddar
- Sliced or diced white onions
- Chopped dill pickles
- Saltines

1. Place the beef in a Dutch oven or large, heavy pot over medium heat. Add the chili seasoning, cumin, garlic, and salt.
2. Cook, stirring occasionally, until browned, 10 to 15 minutes. Add the water and cracker meal and simmer over medium-low heat for 1 hour, or until the flavors meld, stirring occasionally and adjusting the spices as you like.
3. To serve the traditional way: Skim off some of the grease that rises to the surface of the chili as it cooks and toss with the spaghetti noodles. Place a mound of the noodles on each plate and top with the chili, cheese, onions, and pickles. Serve with saltines on the side.

Large-Batch Chili

Double or triple the ingredients, place everything in a slow cooker, and cook on low for 4 to 6 hours, until the flavors meld. Serve or divide among airtight containers and freeze for up to 6 months.

No-Lift White Chicken or Turkey Chili

SERVES 4 TO 6

This creamy, comforting chili tastes like you've been prepping for hours, but you don't even have to pick up a knife! A jar of your favorite green salsa spares you from chopping and sautéing the onions, garlic, and peppers. A carton of cream helps you tame the spice to your liking. Set out an array of garnishes for everyone to help themselves. Sub leftover turkey for the chicken and your post-Thanksgiving feast will feel like a party!

- 3 cups low-sodium chicken broth or homemade turkey stock
- Two 15.5-ounce cans white beans, drained and rinsed
- One 16-ounce jar mild salsa verde
- 1 teaspoon ground cumin
- 3 to 4 cups diced or shredded cooked chicken or turkey (see Hack)
- ⅓ cup heavy cream or half-and-half
- Salt, to taste

FOR SERVING, OPTIONAL

- Diced avocado
- Shredded cheddar or Monterey Jack
- Crushed tortilla chips
- Chopped cilantro
- Jalapeño slices
- Lime wedges
- Sour cream

1. Combine the broth, beans, salsa, and cumin in a medium pot and bring to a boil over high heat.
2. Reduce the heat to medium-low and let simmer, uncovered, for 15 to 20 minutes, until the liquid has reduced by about a third. For a thicker chili, mash some of the beans with a wooden spoon against the side of the pan while it simmers until you get the consistency you're after.
3. Stir in the chicken or turkey and the cream and cook for 3 to 5 minutes longer, until heated through. Taste and adjust the seasoning with salt (but be careful; it's fairly salty as is!).
4. Ladle the chili into soup bowls and serve with your preferred garnishes on the side.

Check out this hack!

HACK: Debone a Rotisserie Chicken in 2 Minutes

If you don't have leftover chicken or turkey, a store-bought rotisserie chicken is a quick solution. Skip the hassle and mess of separating the meat from the bones with this simple hack: As soon as you get home from the store, stick the entire chicken (while it's still warm) in a large heavy-duty freezer bag and massage it with your hands. The skin and bones will just slide off! You won't waste an ounce of the meat this way. If the chicken is cold, warm it up for a minute or two in the microwave. This is important! If it's too hard, the meat won't break apart easily.

Kansas Chicken Soup

SERVES AT LEAST 8

This soup is like a hug in a bowl. Even on hot summer nights, Kid 3's eyes light up when I make it. It's a universal symbol of love when someone makes you chicken noodle soup, and you just feel good when you eat it, too. The chicken and broth are the Diana Ross of this dish, and the carrots are The Supremes, meaning it wouldn't be the same without them. I use whole baby carrots and finger-length pieces of celery that I slice up afterward to add back to the finished soup (or not, depending on the eater). They're the only veggies that survive the long simmer; once the onion, parsley, and garlic have given their all, they get fished out and tossed into the compost. A splash of vinegar adds a touch of brightness you won't want to miss. I let everyone dish their soup up buffet-style, with noodles or rice and assorted veggies in separate bowls for customizing.

CHICKEN BROTH

One 2½- to 3-pound whole chicken

3 or 4 celery stalks, trimmed and cut in thirds

1 large onion, quartered

1 bunch flat-leaf parsley

2 cups baby carrots

¼ cup apple cider vinegar

10 to 20 garlic cloves, peeled

1 tablespoon salt

1 tablespoon peppercorns, tied in cheesecloth or a tea bag

FOR A SOUP STATION

Noodles (homemade or packaged)

Cooked rice

Cooked riced cauliflower

Avocado chunks

Lemon wedges

1. **MAKE THE CHICKEN BROTH:** Place the chicken, celery, onion, parsley, carrots, vinegar, garlic, salt, and peppercorns in a large soup pot, Instant Pot, or slow cooker. Fill with enough water to cover the chicken, leaving several inches at the top to allow for boiling.
2. If using an Instant Pot, hit the "soup" button. If using a slow cooker, cook on low for 6 to 8 hours. If cooking on the stove, bring to a boil, partially cover with the lid, reduce to a simmer, and cook for 1½ to 3 hours, until the chicken is very tender and falling off the bone.
3. Fish out the carrots and celery with a slotted spoon and slice them into bite-size pieces. Transfer the chicken to a cutting board, remove the skin and bones, and cut the meat into bite-size pieces.
4. Strain the broth, discard any remaining solids, and return the broth to the pot along with the cut-up chicken.
5. **TO SERVE:** Set up a soup station with noodles or rice, riced cauliflower, the cooked carrots and celery, avocado chunks, and lemon wedges. Let everyone serve themselves!

Storage Tip

After the soup cools down, freeze the leftovers in airtight containers for up to 6 months. I sometimes freeze the broth separately for making homemade noodles or dumplings like the ones I grew up on in Kansas (see Tre's Homemade Noodles in Chicken Broth, page 110).

Tre's Homemade Noodles in Chicken Broth

SERVES AT LEAST 8

When I was growing up in Kansas, having chicken and homemade egg noodles every week was like Taco Tuesday here in California. Everyone knows what they are, and if they don't make them, they know the day of the week a local restaurant does. My aunt Ona used to make noodles for hundreds of customers each week at a popular local restaurant called Red Barn. Whenever I'd visit her, the noodles would be draped over the backs of her kitchen chairs and on the kitchen table. Since they're handmade, they're not uniform in size; some noodles are thicker than others (and the thick ones were always my favorite!). My sister Tre (short for Teresa) gave me her recipe card for making a family-size batch of these rich, eggy noodles. They're not hard, but they do take a little extra time and muscle. As someone who watches my carbs closely, I make them as an occasional treat.

- 2 cups all-purpose flour, plus more for dusting
- 1 tablespoon salt
- 1 large egg
- 3 large egg yolks
- 3 to 4 tablespoons cold water, or more, as needed, divided
- Few drops of yellow food coloring, optional
- 8 to 12 cups Chicken Broth (see page 109)

1. Combine the flour and salt in a large bowl and make a well in the center. Add the egg and egg yolks to the well along with 2 tablespoons of the water and the food coloring, if using.
2. Beat the eggs with a fork, mixing in the flour and adding water a tablespoonful at a time, and knead the dough just enough to bring it together to form a sticky ball.
3. Cover and let the dough rest for 10 minutes. Dust a work surface with flour, dump the dough onto the surface, and form into a ball. Knead enough flour into the dough so it no longer sticks to your hands but is still slightly damp.
4. Cut the dough into four equal sections and roll out each one with a rolling pin to ¼ to ⅛ inch thickness (I like mine on the thicker side). Cut into strips with a sharp knife or pizza cutter.
5. Pour the broth into a large pot and bring to a boil. Add the noodles and cook until tender, 10 to 20 minutes, depending on the thickness of the noodle. Or let them dry on the countertop and then transfer them to plastic bags to refrigerate for up to 3 days or freeze for up to 6 months.

Chicken and Noodles over Mashed Potatoes

Yes, this really is a thing! As a Kansas kid, the notion of pouring chicken and noodles over mashed potatoes seems normal. It doesn't dawn on you that you're eating a starch over a starch; you just know you love it. It's hearty, it's comforting, it's warm, and if you think about it, it's two of just about anyone's favorite things: noodles and mashed potatoes! You can use my recipe, The Fluffiest Mashed Potatoes (page 132) or your own. It's not exactly health food, but for me, it's a surefire cure for homesickness. Just place the potatoes in a bowl, add a ladleful of chicken soup and noodles, and eat!

STAUB

Meatball and Veggie Soup

SERVES 4

One of my favorite "use what you have" meals is actually a soup. My mom's vegetable soup with "hamburger balls" is made by seasoning ground beef with Magic Seasoning, pinching off bits of the beef, rolling it into balls, and then dropping them in a pot of boiling water flavored with bouillon cubes and whatever vegetable tidbits you have lying around in the fridge or freezer. My version relies on pre-made meatballs and frozen veggies, and is an excellent vehicle for my Tomato Flavor Bombs (page 29).

- One 32-ounce container low-sodium beef broth
- One 14.5-ounce can diced tomatoes
- 3 Tomato Flavor Bombs (page 29, or see Note)
- 2 celery stalks, diced
- 1 small onion, diced
- 12 to 16 ounces frozen precooked Italian-style meatballs
- One 12-ounce bag mixed frozen vegetables (such as carrots, green beans, corn, and peas)
- Magic Seasoning (page 28) or salt and pepper, to taste
- Cooked macaroni or rice, optional
- Grated Parmesan, optional

1. Place the broth, diced tomatoes, Flavor Bombs, celery, and onions in a large soup pot and bring to a boil over high heat, stirring to blend.
2. Add the meatballs. Reduce the heat to a low simmer, uncovered, and cook for 20 minutes, or until the meatballs are heated through.
3. Add the vegetables and cook for 5 minutes, or until heated through. Taste and adjust the seasoning.
4. Place macaroni or rice in bowls, if desired, and then ladle the soup on top. Serve and pass the Parmesan at the table if you'd like.

Note

If you don't have Tomato Flavor Bombs handy in your freezer, use 3 tablespoons tomato paste plus ¾ teaspoon minced garlic and 1 teaspoon dried basil, Italian seasoning, or oregano.

Lasagna Soup

SERVES 4 TO 6

A pan of lasagna is a lot of work and super time-consuming. In Kansas, we didn't have a ton of Italian restaurants, but we did have a local restaurant that would make lasagna one day a week (see: time-consuming). Lasagna is usually a lot of food as well. It's hard to serve for a family of four unless you plan on having it a few nights that week. This soup is an easy way to get your lasagna fix, even if you skip the pasta. And it's easy to store and eat throughout the week. Lasagna noodles work great but aren't a must (I find leftover corkscrew pasta to be easier to work with, anyway).

- 1 pound ground meat of choice or plant-based substitute
- 1 small onion, finely chopped
- One 32-ounce container chicken or beef broth
- One 24-ounce jar marinara sauce
- One 14.5-ounce can diced tomatoes
- 2 teaspoons Magic Seasoning (page 28)
- 1½ teaspoons chopped garlic
- 3 to 4 cups cooked pasta of choice
- 1 cup heavy cream

FOR SERVING

- Ricotta
- Grated mozzarella
- Grated Parmesan

Stovetop

1. Place the meat and onion in a large pot. Cook over medium-high heat, breaking up the meat with a wooden spoon and stirring occasionally, until the onion is tender and the meat is cooked through, 8 to 10 minutes.
2. Add the broth, marinara, tomatoes, Magic Seasoning, and garlic and bring to a boil. Then reduce the heat to medium-low and continue to cook until the flavors have melded, 30 to 40 minutes. Stir in the pasta and cream and cook for 5 more minutes, or just long enough to heat through.
3. Garnish each serving with a scoop of ricotta and sprinkles of mozzarella and Parmesan.

Slow Cooker

1. Place the meat, onion, broth, marinara, tomatoes, Magic Seasoning, and garlic in a slow cooker, breaking up the meat with a spoon, and cook on high for 3 to 4 hours, until the flavors are melded.
2. Stir in the pasta and cream and cook for 5 more minutes, or just long enough to heat through.
3. Garnish each serving with a scoop of ricotta and sprinkles of mozzarella and Parmesan.

CHAPTER 3

Simple Sides

We are a family of unapologetic carnivores, but I always try to make sure we all get a balanced diet. But vegetables aren't always the easiest sell around here. We're all, shall we say, highly selective about the ones we'll eat, and if I'm being honest, the grown-ups are as guilty as the kids. (Scooter hates mushrooms, and if a sliver of bell pepper winds up on my plate, it will be raked to the side.) Through trial and error, I've figured out the best ways to get us all to eat our veggies. Some turn up in whole-meal recipes in the previous chapters, such as my Meatball and Veggie Soup (page 113) or Pesto-Glazed Salmon with Roasted Asparagus and Cherry Tomatoes (page 74). The recipes in this chapter are the ones I turn to when an entrée cries for the company of a no-frills salad or a simple hot veggie or starch to round out the plate. I've also included a few quick favorites for the breadbasket.

"Serve Yourself" Simple Butter Lettuce Salad

SERVES 4

Italy has some of the best food I've had anywhere in the world. Their produce is incredible! Turns out, when you're working with a good base, you don't need to complicate it. I can't remember one fancy, overly done salad dressing I ever had while our family was on vacation there. It's truly just olive oil and balsamic—that's it! This salad is simple but perfect: two parts EVOO to one part balsamic vinegar over tender butter lettuce, seasoned with salt and pepper, and sometimes with optional additions in little bowls on the side. This style of serving salad works extremely well at home with my picky-eating family. I set out the lightly dressed lettuce and let everyone help themselves to whatever extras they wish.

- 2 medium heads butter lettuce, washed and dried well
- 2 tablespoons extra-virgin olive oil, or more, to taste
- 1 tablespoon balsamic vinegar, or more, to taste
- 8 grinds coarse salt (I use pink Himalayan)
- 4 grinds black pepper
- Flaky sea salt

FOR SERVING, OPTIONAL

- Avocado chunks
- Sliced cucumber
- Olives
- Sliced scallions
- Cherry tomatoes
- Toasted sliced or slivered almonds
- Croutons
- Shaved Parmesan

1. Roughly chop or tear the lettuce into bite-size pieces and place in a large salad bowl.
2. Right before serving, mix the oil, vinegar, coarse salt, and pepper in a small bowl, drizzle over the lettuce, and toss well to coat. Taste, and if it needs more dressing, just mix up some more, keeping with the two parts oil to one part vinegar ratio.
3. Serve in a large salad bowl surrounded by small bowls of flaky salt and desired toppings and let everyone dress their salads as they wish.

HACK: Lettuce

If I'm buying bagged or boxed spring mix or other tender lettuces, I always put a piece of paper towel in with it after I open it. This helps keep the lettuce from turning slimy by absorbing excess moisture and condensation. If I'm buying a head of lettuce, I core, wash, and dry the leaves (usually in my salad spinner) and store it wrapped in a paper towel in a loose baggie. Or if I have long spears of romaine, I trim the bottoms and store in a tall flower vase with a little water on the bottom to keep them crisp longer. I loosely cover with a baggie and put it in the fridge until ready to use.

Mom's Marinated Cucumbers and Onions

MAKES ABOUT 1 QUART

Many of us who grew up in the Midwest or the South with cucumbers coming out our eyeballs in the summertime have memories of standing with the refrigerator door open, snacking on these tangy treats right out of the jar or bowl! I do it to this day. I try to have a batch on hand all summer long if we need something cool and crunchy to go along with something off the grill.

- 2 or 3 medium cucumbers, peeled and thinly sliced into rounds
- 1 medium white or red onion, thinly sliced into half-moons
- 2 teaspoons salt, or to taste
- 1 cup ice
- 2 tablespoons sugar, or to taste
- ½ cup white vinegar or apple cider vinegar
- ½ cup water

1. Place the cucumbers and onion in a large bowl, sprinkle with salt, and then add the ice and just enough water to cover. Let soak for about 30 minutes. (This will make the cukes crispier.)
2. Drain in a colander and remove the ice cubes. Transfer the cucumber and onion to a clean glass jar or bowl (I always put mine in a Pyrex dish with a lid).
3. Sprinkle with the sugar and cover with the vinegar and ½ cup water, making sure all the cucumbers and onions are submerged. If not, add more vinegar and water, keeping a roughly 50/50 ratio. Cover and refrigerate for at least an hour, or until very cold. These will last for days! The longer they sit, the better they get! But trust me, you will eat them before that.

Creamy and Tangy Coleslaw

SERVES 8

This simple slaw tastes just the way we make it back home in Kansas. It adds the perfect cooling crunch to tuck into a barbecue sandwich or chili dog or serve alongside fried chicken or anything off the grill.

- ½ cup mayonnaise
- 3 tablespoons apple cider vinegar
- 1 tablespoon sugar, or sweetener to taste (I use NuNaturals stevia simple syrup or stevia drops)
- 1 teaspoon Magic Seasoning (page 28)
- ½ teaspoon celery seeds
- One 16-ounce bag coleslaw mix
- Salt and pepper

1. Whisk together the mayonnaise, vinegar, sugar, Magic Seasoning, and celery seeds in a small bowl.
2. Place the coleslaw mix in a large bowl, cover with the dressing, sprinkle with salt and pepper, and stir well to coat. Taste and adjust the salt, pepper, and sweetener to your liking.
3. Cover the bowl and chill in the refrigerator until ready to serve, ideally for at least an hour to allow the flavors to meld. The slaw may wilt a bit, but it will be good for several days in the refrigerator.

Fast and Frugal Marinated Asparagus

SERVES 4 TO 6

When I moved to California in 1990, two things shocked me: dessert trays or carts at every restaurant and fresh vegetables everywhere! Kansas is far from the land of perennial avocados and oranges, so our produce was spotty at best and highly dependent on the local growing season. Canned vegetables weren't just budget options—most of the year, they were the only option. This recipe was born of that era and is still a keeper to this day. It's tangy, refreshing, and budget-friendly, and it can be thrown together at a moment's notice any time of year, with items straight out of your pantry.

- Two 15-ounce cans asparagus spears
- ½ cup honey
- ½ cup avocado oil or other neutral oil
- ½ cup white vinegar
- 1 teaspoon dry mustard or 1 tablespoon yellow mustard
- ½ teaspoon salt

1. Drain the asparagus and place in a glass dish.
2. Place the honey, oil, vinegar, mustard, and salt in a small saucepan and bring to a boil.
3. Pour the mixture over the asparagus, let cool completely, and then cover with plastic wrap and refrigerate for at least 2 hours or overnight. Serve cold.

Roasted Cherry Tomatoes

MAKES ABOUT 2 CUPS

I always buy the largest container of cherry tomatoes I can get, especially if they're on sale at Costco. I never have to worry about them shriveling up before we can eat them all now that I know the secret to extending their shelf life: roasting them until their skins burst and turn brown, which concentrates their naturally sweet, tangy flavor. They're so delicious and make a great side dish that goes with just about anything. Fold them into pasta or rice, heap them on toast, mix them with other tender veggies, or use them in my Spaghetti Squash Casserole Hack (page 131).

- 2 pints (4 cups) cherry tomatoes, cut in half if desired
- 1 tablespoon avocado oil or olive oil (or spray)
- Magic Seasoning (page 28) or salt and pepper, to taste
- 3 to 4 fresh thyme or rosemary sprigs, optional
- Balsamic glaze, optional

Oven Method

1. Preheat the oven to 375°F. Line a baking sheet with parchment paper. Toss the tomatoes with the oil and Magic Seasoning. Spread them out in a single layer on the baking sheet. Add the thyme, if using.
2. Roast for 25 to 30 minutes, until the tomatoes are caramelized and start to burst.
3. Serve hot or at room temperature as a side dish, drizzled with balsamic glaze, if using.

Air Fryer Method

1. Preheat the air fryer to 400°F. Toss the tomatoes with the oil and Magic Seasoning.
2. Spread out the tomatoes in the air fryer basket. Add the thyme, if using, and air-fry for 8 to 10 minutes, or until the tomatoes are caramelized and start to burst.
3. Serve hot or at room temperature as a side dish, drizzled with balsamic glaze, if using.

Storage Tip

They'll keep in the fridge in a covered container for about 5 days, or in the freezer in an airtight container or freezer bag for up to 3 months.

Savory Kale Chips

SERVES 6

If you want to get a picky eater to try something new, figure out a way to turn it into a chip! My family would never try kale on its own, but they can't stop eating these. While they're great as a snack or a sub for chips if you're having a sandwich, I usually serve these as a veggie side with dinner. And they're low-carb! Ninety-nine percent of the time, I'll just sprinkle my Magic Seasoning (page 28) on them, but you can use any seasoning you want here: ranch, taco, Cajun—the list goes on and on. Mom tip: Make sure you remove the leaves from the stems.

- 1 bunch kale or one 6-ounce bag chopped kale
- 1 tablespoon avocado oil or olive oil (or spray)
- Magic Seasoning (page 28) or seasoning of choice, to taste

1. Preheat the oven to 300°F. Line a baking sheet with parchment paper. Remove the kale leaves from the thick stems with a sharp knife or kitchen shears.
2. Spread the kale on the baking sheet, drizzle or spray lightly with oil, and sprinkle with Magic Seasoning.
3. Place in the oven and roast for 20 to 30 minutes, tossing every 10 minutes, until crisp. They should be browned around the edges but not burnt.

Storage Tip

If you're not serving the chips immediately, cool completely and store in an airtight container, with paper towels to prevent sogginess, in a cool, dry place away from direct sunlight for up to 5 days. Or store in the fridge for a few days longer. If needed, re-crisp in the oven or air fryer for a few minutes.

BOTTLED AT SOURCE
355 mL
(12 FL OZ)
MINERAL

Perfectly Roasted Spaghetti Squash

SERVES 2 TO 4

Spaghetti squash is an inexpensive, low-carb, super-nutritious veggie that magically forms noodle-like strands as it cooks. It's mild enough that, if it's doctored up just a little, even a picky kid might eat it. But how many times have you walked past it at the grocery store thinking, *I just don't have the time for that one today*? That used to be me, too! The thing holding me back was always the daunting task of trying to cut the thing open. Turns out we don't need to cut it at all! This is one of my favorite food hacks of all time: Just poke that baby with a fork or sharp knife and stick it in the oven. When it's done it will cut like butter, I promise. I love spaghetti squash as a side veggie. Make it a main dish by ladling meatballs simmered in your favorite pasta sauce right over the top or try the hack below.

1 medium spaghetti squash (2 to 4 pounds)

FOR SERVING, OPTIONAL

Simple: Butter, flaky salt, and/or Magic Seasoning (page 28)

Sweet: Brown sugar, honey, or maple syrup

Savory: Herbs, grated Parmesan, pesto, meatballs (page 70), and/or pasta sauce

Watch me make this!

1. Preheat the oven to 375°F. Line a baking sheet with parchment paper.
2. Pierce the skin of the squash in a few places with a fork or a sharp knife to allow steam to escape. Set the squash on the baking sheet and place on the center rack of the oven.
3. Roast for about 1 hour, flipping halfway through, until the squash is soft enough to make a dent but not mushy when pressed with your finger (be careful not to burn yourself!).
4. Remove the squash from the oven and let cool and then cut lengthwise from end to end. Scoop out the seeds and inner fibers with a spoon and discard. Use a fork to gently fluff and separate the spaghetti strands from the shells. Leave them in the shells to serve or scrape them into a bowl and mix with desired ingredients for serving.
5. Store in halves or shredded into a container for up to 5 days in the fridge. Rewarm in a skillet with a little oil or butter over medium-low heat until hot, in a 350°F oven, or in a microwave until just hot. Don't overcook it!

HACK: Spaghetti Squash Casserole

Two hacks = one fabulous vegetarian main: While your spaghetti squash is roasting, slide a pan of cherry tomatoes on the lower oven rack with a little oil and seasonings for the last half hour or pop them in your air fryer as directed in the recipe for Roasted Cherry Tomatoes (page 127). You can turn both into a rib-sticking, flavor-packed vegetarian entrée in less than 10 minutes with one secret weapon to tie them together: Boursin Garlic & Fine Herbs cheese. One disc of this soft, pre-seasoned spread provides the perfect amount of creaminess and spice. Coat a 2-quart baking dish with nonstick cooking spray, scrape the strands of the spaghetti squash into the dish, and then spread the tomatoes on top. Push the mixture in the center with a spoon to form a hole large enough to fit the Boursin disc and set it inside. Drizzle with a little olive oil over the cheese and bake in the preheated 375°F oven for 10 minutes, or until the cheese is heated through. Remove from the oven, stir the hot cheese through the mixture, and garnish with basil. Season with sea salt and drizzle with a little more oil, if desired.

The Fluffiest Mashed Potatoes

SERVES 6 TO 8

As a kid, I remember learning how to peel potatoes. It was fun for a few minutes, but then very quickly it turned into work! The peeling was a necessary evil to get to the heavenly mashed results . . . or so we thought. Then a few years ago, I heard about this technique of pushing cooked potatoes through the grates of a crosshatch wire rack to bypass the dreaded peeling. I had to give it a try. To simplify the process even further, I first boiled the potatoes whole, without even poking them with a fork. And sister, talk about a game changer! I posted a video titled "No Peel Mashed Potato Hack" and quickly realized pretty much everyone else in the world felt like I did about peeling potatoes. The video has been viewed tens of millions of times since and helped put LORAfied on the map. This recipe shows how I incorporate the technique into what may be the lowest lift, biggest payoff mashed potato recipe out there. To achieve maximum fluffiness without messing with a food mill or ricer, I find my handy-dandy electric hand mixer does the job perfectly.

3 to 4 pounds Yukon Gold potatoes

1 tablespoon plus 1 teaspoon salt, divided, plus more for serving

⅓ cup (⅔ stick) salted butter, melted, plus more for serving

1 cup half-and-half, warmed

Black pepper, optional

Chives, optional

1. Place a crosshatch wire rack on top of a large bowl.
2. Place the potatoes in a large pot and cover with about 2 inches of water. Add about 1 tablespoon salt to the water and bring it to a boil over high heat. Boil for 20 to 30 minutes, until you can easily insert a toothpick in the center of a potato.
3. Drain the potatoes. Once they are cool enough to handle, slice them in half lengthwise. Place the potatoes cut-side down on the wire rack and press them with your hands (or with the bottom of a glass if they're still too hot) so that the flesh falls through the grates into the bowl, leaving the skins behind. Discard the skins.
4. Add the melted butter and 1 teaspoon salt to the bowl and then, with an electric hand mixer on low speed, gradually add the half-and-half (you may not need all of it) and beat just until creamy, 1 or 2 minutes. Take care not to overbeat; it's better to have a few lumps than gluey potatoes!
5. Taste for seasoning and serve with more butter, salt, pepper, and chives, if desired.

HACK: Shortcut Baked Potato

How would you like to have a baked potato in half the time? Crispy skin, fluffy inside, but without the hour wait in the oven? Give those spuds a head start in the microwave.

Preheat the oven to 425°F. Scrub one to four russet or sweet potatoes under running water, pat them dry, and prick in several places with a fork.

Place them in a microwave-safe dish and microwave on high for 5 minutes; flip and microwave for 5 more minutes. Rub the potatoes all over with avocado oil or olive oil and sprinkle generously with salt.

Set the potatoes on the middle rack of the oven. (Place a parchment-lined baking sheet underneath the potatoes to catch any juices). Roast for 10 to 20 minutes, depending on the size of the potato, or until the skins are crisp and dry and the flesh can be easily pierced with a fork. Cut the potatoes in half lengthwise and add butter, salt, and pepper, or whatever toppings you like.

Parmesan-Crusted Cabbage Steaks
with Balsamic Drizzle

SERVES 4

Even if the only way you're willing to eat cabbage is shredded in slaw, you just might learn to love cooked cabbage if you try it this way. These "steaks" are not only packed with savory goodness, they're also hearty enough to serve as a vegetarian main.

- 1 medium head purple or green cabbage
- 2 tablespoons avocado oil or cooking spray
- Magic Seasoning (page 28), to taste
- 3 or 4 tablespoons grated Parmesan, optional
- Balsamic glaze, to taste

1. Preheat the oven to 450°F. Line a baking sheet with parchment paper. Peel off and discard the loose outer leaves of the cabbage.
2. Set the cabbage head on a cutting board and slice lengthwise into ¾-inch "steaks." Lay the pieces on the baking sheet and brush both sides with the oil.
3. Season the steaks lightly with Magic Seasoning. Roast for 15 minutes and then flip them over and roast for another 10 to 15 minutes, until they pierce easily with a knife. If using Parmesan, sprinkle the steaks and return to the oven during the last 5 minutes, or bake until the cheese is melted and lightly browned.
4. Remove the steaks from the oven and drizzle with the balsamic glaze.

Roasted Honey-Dijon Brussels Sprouts

SERVES 4

There's an old line my mom said a lot—"the devil is in the details"—and boy does it apply to brussels sprouts! If they're prepared the wrong way, you'll never want to try them again, but when you make them *this way*, you'll have folks asking for seconds! If the last time you tried brussels sprouts, they were waterlogged and covered in sauce, these are a must try! Forget everything you thought you knew about these guys and get ready to fall in love with a veggie!

2 tablespoons avocado oil
2 tablespoons honey
2 tablespoons Dijon mustard
1 pound brussels sprouts, trimmed and halved
Magic Seasoning (page 28), to taste

1. Preheat the oven to 400°F. Line a baking sheet with parchment.
2. Place the oil, honey, and mustard in a medium bowl and whisk until well blended. Add the sprouts, toss to coat, and spread them out on the baking sheet. Sprinkle with the Magic Seasoning.
3. Roast for 20 to 25 minutes, until tender and browned.

Crispy, Cheesy, Smashed, and Roasted Broccoli

SERVES 4

I never imagined I would succeed in getting my finicky kids to devour whole plates of broccoli! Then I tried this genius method of steaming and smashing the florets before roasting. The broccoli turns tender and then—once flattened and showered with Parm or my favorite, pecorino Romano—it evenly browns and turns crispy in the oven. I add a little paprika and Magic Seasoning for extra zip. Ranch seasoning or taco seasoning will also raise the enthusiasm level. Mind blown!

- 4 cups broccoli florets
- 2 to 3 tablespoons water
- Avocado oil spray
- 1 teaspoon Magic Seasoning (page 28)
- ½ teaspoon paprika, optional
- ¼ cup grated Parmesan or pecorino Romano

1. Preheat the oven to 425°F. Line a baking sheet with parchment paper.
2. Place the broccoli in a microwave-safe bowl and add the water. Cover with a lid or a small plate and cook in the microwave on high for 3 minutes, or until tender.
3. Drain the broccoli and then spread it out on the baking sheet and flatten each floret with the bottom of a glass. (If the broccoli doesn't easily flatten, microwave for another 30 seconds or so.) Spray with the avocado oil, season with the Magic Seasoning and paprika, and then sprinkle with the cheese.
4. Roast in the oven for about 15 minutes, or until crispy.

Old-School Green Beans with Bacon

SERVES 8

The green veggie of my childhood! When I moved to California from Kansas, one of the first things I had to figure out was my mom's green beans. Whether you make this recipe with fresh, canned, or frozen beans, they are life-changing. It's wild, because it tastes like there are layers upon layers to this recipe, but in reality, it's made with a handful of truly simple ingredients. While I like my beans cooked until they're soft, I know most folks prefer to have a little crunch to 'em. No matter which side of the beanstalk you're on, you are going to love these! And yes, they can be made vegetarian: Just take out the bacon and sub vegetable stock for the chicken stock.

- 2 pounds fresh or frozen green beans, washed and trimmed
- 1 cup chopped bacon (about 8 slices), divided
- ½ large red or yellow onion, thinly sliced or chopped
- 1 garlic clove, minced
- 2 teaspoons Magic Seasoning (page 28)
- 2 cups chicken broth

Slow Cooker Method

1. Place the green beans, half the bacon, and the onion, garlic, Magic Seasoning, and broth in the slow cooker.
2. Cover and cook on high for 4 hours, or on low for 8 hours, stirring a few times during cooking, for soft, fork-tender beans. (If you like your beans firmer, check the beans an hour or two sooner.)
3. Meanwhile, cook the remaining bacon in a small skillet over medium heat until the fat has rendered and the bacon is browned and crispy, 5 to 7 minutes. Drain on paper towels.
4. Transfer the beans to a serving dish, top with the cooked bacon bits, and serve.

Stovetop Method

1. Cook all of the bacon in a large, deep skillet with a lid over medium heat until it begins to release its fat (see Tip). Then add the onion, garlic, and Magic Seasoning and continue to cook and stir until the onions are soft and the bacon is browned, 5 to 7 minutes.
2. Add the green beans to the pan, toss to coat, and then pour in enough broth to almost cover the beans. Bring the mixture to a simmer, cover with a lid, and cook until the beans reach your desired tenderness.

Tip

We love this cooked in all the bacon fat, but I understand if you'd rather not. If you prefer, you can cook the bacon until it's crispy and drain it on a paper towel–lined plate, remove all but a couple of tablespoons of the grease before adding the onion, garlic, and seasoning, and stir in the cooked bacon at the end.

Storage Tip

It's best to allow the cornbread to thaw slowly and evenly in the refrigerator overnight before reheating. **To reheat in the oven:** Place on a baking sheet, cover loosely with foil, and reheat at 350°F for 10 to 15 minutes, until warmed through. **To reheat in the air fryer:** Reheat for 2 or 3 minutes at 325°F. **To reheat in the microwave:** Wrap in a damp paper towel and microwave on high for 20 to 30 seconds.

Copycat Marie Callender's Cornbread with Honey Butter

SERVES 10 TO 12

I'll never forget my first trip to Hollywood—nor will I forget my first taste of Marie Callender's famous cornbread. It was the summer of 1983. My mom had been to Los Angeles many times and was a big fan of Marie Callender's Restaurant & Bakery, a chain of homestyle restaurants that started in Orange County, California, in the 1960s. Marie's cornbread was really more like a slice of unfrosted cake. I'd never seen anything like it! So I wasn't shocked when my mom leaned over and said, "You know their secret is cake mix added to the batter." Many years later, I tried Marie Callender's cornbread mix that's now sold in supermarkets and knew instantly that it wasn't the same. I remembered my mom's tip and decided to try mixing cornbread batter with cake batter to see what would happen. Sure enough, Norma Jean was right! To fully recreate that restaurant memory, I whipped up some honey butter to go with it.

CAKE BATTER

Nonstick cooking spray

One 13.25- to 15.25-ounce box yellow cake mix

1 cup water

⅓ cup avocado oil

3 large eggs

CORNBREAD BATTER

One 8.5-ounce box Jiffy Corn Muffin mix

⅓ cup milk

1 large egg

HONEY BUTTER

4 tablespoons (½ stick) butter, softened (I always use salted, but it really doesn't matter)

¼ cup honey

1. Cover an oven rack with a sheet of foil and set it on the top level of the oven to prevent overbrowning. Set another rack in the middle.
2. Preheat the oven to 350°F. Spray a 9 x 13-inch baking pan with cooking spray.
3. **MAKE THE CAKE BATTER:** Following the package directions, combine the cake mix, water, oil, and eggs in a large bowl with an electric hand mixer set on medium speed, or beat vigorously with a big spoon or a rubber spatula, for about 2 minutes, or until blended.
4. **MAKE THE CORNBREAD BATTER:** Following the package directions, combine the corn muffin mix, milk, and egg in a medium bowl with an electric hand mixer set on medium speed, or beat vigorously with a big spoon or a rubber spatula, for about 30 seconds, just long enough to incorporate (a few lumps are okay—don't overmix).
5. Pour the cornbread batter into the cake batter and stir until combined. Pour into the prepared pan and place on the middle rack. Bake for 30 to 40 minutes, until a toothpick inserted in the center comes out clean.
6. **MAKE THE HONEY BUTTER:** While the cornbread bakes, blend the butter and honey in a food processor or blender, or whisk in a small bowl. Transfer to a small bowl for serving.
7. Cut the cornbread into squares and serve hot, with the honey butter on the side. Or wrap the squares individually in plastic wrap and freeze for up to 3 months.

Corn Muffins

Pour the batter into a 12-cup and a 6-cup muffin pan lined with cupcake liners. Bake for 13 to 15 minutes, until a toothpick inserted in the center comes out clean. (Makes about 18 muffins.)

Butter Swim Biscuits

MAKES ABOUT 9

If you love biscuits but don't like to bake, these are for you! They are that easy. I ate biscuits and gravy almost every morning as a child. I would have two biscuits, cracked open with gravy, with a side of ham and hash browns—remember, we're talking Kansas here! When it comes to biscuits, I'm an equal opportunity eater! I love them all: buttermilk, canned, drop, rolled . . . you name it. But without question, these are *the best* and *easiest* biscuits I have ever made! Just five ingredients plus a lil' salt.

½ cup (1 stick) melted butter
2½ cups all-purpose flour
4 teaspoons baking powder
1 tablespoon sugar
2 teaspoons salt
2 cups buttermilk or whole milk

1. Preheat the oven to 450°F. Pour the butter into an 8-inch square baking pan.
2. Mix the flour, baking powder, sugar, and salt in a medium bowl. Stir in the milk with a large spoon until just combined, making sure not to overmix the batter. (It should be lumpy.)
3. Drop the batter on top of the melted butter and spread it out to the edges of the pan. Cut the batter in the pan with a sharp knife into nine squares so some of the butter seeps between the biscuits.
4. Bake for 18 to 25 minutes, until a toothpick inserted in the center comes out clean. Let the butter soak into the biscuits for a few minutes before breaking into squares and serving.

Storage Tip

These are best hot out of the oven, but once cooled, they can be covered and stored at room temperature for up to 3 days. Leftover biscuits can be wrapped individually in plastic wrap and stored in a zip-top bag in the freezer for up to 3 months. Thaw at room temperature for about 30 minutes and reheat in a 350°F oven for about 10 minutes, or until warmed through.

CHAPTER 4

Whole-Meal Salads and Bowls

When someone says "salad," what do you think of? Honestly, before I moved to Los Angeles, my mind would swing from iceberg lettuce to Jell-O molds that crossed into dessert territory! In Kansas, the definition of "salad" was very broad and, unless it was a holiday or a potluck, it was most likely super boring. But in LA, which is the salad capital of the world (well, at least I think it is), it's pretty hard to find a restaurant without a salad—and I mean a really good salad: fresh, light, and made with all of California's great homegrown produce by LA's hottest, most creative chefs. I love it all! In the Simple Sides chapter (starting on page 117), I shared a few simple salad sidekicks to round out a meal. In this chapter, salads (and salad-adjacent concoctions) are the meal—hearty enough for a family supper or light enough for a ladies' lunch or an easy meal for one when the rest of the family is away. And for those times when most of your day is spent driving from one place to another, I've even included a low-carb salad trick you can make in your car in the fast-food parking lot: Drive-Thru Cheeseburger Salad (page 157).

Waldorf-Inspired Chicken Salad

SERVES 4

During my years as a single mom working long hours as a rookie television reporter, I often stretched two diced-up chicken breasts into five lunches or late-night suppers for myself in the form of this salad (or some variation, depending on what I had on hand). I love it to this day. It's based on a Waldorf salad, which typically consists of apples, celery, grapes, nuts, and mayo. Back then, I rarely had celery and grapes in the crisper, so I left those out and tossed in dried cranberries for bursts of tangy sweetness instead. But if you have 'em, by all means use 'em! A little chopped red onion or scallions won't hurt either. Feel free to lighten it up by subbing yogurt for some of the mayo. Serve on a lettuce leaf if you want to get fancy.

- 2 cooked boneless, skinless chicken breasts, diced (about 2 cups)
- 1 apple (preferably green), cored and diced
- ½ to 1 cup mayonnaise or unsweetened plain yogurt, or half mayo and half yogurt
- ½ cup coarsely chopped walnuts, toasted if desired
- ¼ cup dried cranberries, optional
- Squeeze of lemon juice or splash of vinegar (any kind), if needed
- Salt and pepper, to taste

1. Combine the chicken, apple, mayonnaise, walnuts, and cranberries, if using, in a large bowl and stir to combine.
2. Taste and add a squeeze of lemon juice to sharpen the flavor if needed, and season to taste with salt and pepper.
3. Refrigerate in a covered container for up to 4 days.

HACK: Quick-Poaching Chicken Breast

If you don't already have some cooked chicken on hand, here's the best way to cook it so it will be moist and tender and not dry and tasteless. Place two large boneless, skinless chicken breasts in a large saucepan with a quart of cold water, or just enough to cover it by about 2 inches—no more! Season with a tablespoon of salt and bring to a gentle boil over medium heat. Flip the chicken breasts with tongs, cover tightly with a lid, remove the pan from the heat, and let the chicken continue to poach in the hot water for 10 to 20 minutes longer, until an instant-read thermometer registers 165°F in the thickest part of the meat. Remove from the water and let rest for about 5 minutes to let the juices redistribute before slicing.

Chicken, Grapefruit, and Butter Lettuce Salad à la Amy's

SERVES 4

Los Angeles is the salad capital of the world and quite possibly the Chinese chicken salad capital of the world as well! There are probably thousands of restaurants in the LA area offering some version, but Amy's Grapefruit Salad, a menu favorite of the iconic Stanley's Restaurant in the Valley, is among the best! If you want to feel like you're having lunch in Hollywood, this is the one to make. Warning: You may want to wear sunglasses while eating it. Serve with iced tea and a lemon wedge . . . that's the power move. For my interpretation, I slice the fresh grapefruit into bite-size pieces rather than attempting to cut out individual sections. I think it's prettier that way—not to mention less finicky!

TAMARI SESAME DRESSING

¼ cup avocado oil

¼ cup tamari or low-sodium soy sauce

¼ cup rice vinegar

1 tablespoon honey or sugar, or to taste

1 tablespoon sesame seeds, toasted if desired

1 teaspoon grated fresh garlic or ½ teaspoon garlic powder, optional

1 teaspoon grated ginger or ½ teaspoon ground ginger, optional

Salt and pepper, to taste

SALAD

1 ruby red or pink grapefruit

2 medium heads butter lettuce, washed and dried well

1 avocado, peeled, seeded, and cut into chunks

1 cup shredded cooked chicken (see Hack: Debone a Rotisserie Chicken in Two Minutes, page 106)

½ cup Asian-style crunchy rice noodles (such as La Choy)

¼ cup cashews or toasted slivered almonds

Flaky sea salt, optional

2 tablespoons toasted sesame seeds, optional

1. **MAKE THE DRESSING:** Place the oil, tamari, vinegar, honey, sesame seeds, and garlic and ginger, if using, in a small bowl and whisk to blend. (Or place all the ingredients in a small jar with a tight lid and shake until blended.) Season to taste with salt and pepper. Add a little more sweetener, if desired.
2. **MAKE THE SALAD:** Peel the grapefruit and trim off the outer white pith. Cut crosswise into ¼-inch slices and then into bite-size wedges.
3. Roughly chop or tear the lettuce into bite-size pieces and place into a large bowl. Add the avocado, chicken, and grapefruit pieces.
4. Drizzle the salad with about half the dressing and toss to coat. Add the rice noodles and cashews and toss again. Taste and add a little more dressing and, if desired, a sprinkle of sea salt and sesame seeds. Serve.
5. Store any leftover dressing in an airtight container in the refrigerator for up to 2 weeks; bring to room temperature and shake well before using.

Rick Spring-Field Salad
with Strawberries, Feta, and Creamy Poppy Seed Dressing

SERVES 4 (MAKES 1⅓ CUPS DRESSING)

My love for Rick Springfield started in August of '81. "Jessie's Girl" was number 1 on the radio and Dr. Noah Drake was number 1 in our hearts on *General Hospital*. Photos of him clipped from *Tiger Beat* and *Teen Beat* covered my bedroom walls like wallpaper. Album after album, I knew the words to every song, went to all the concerts, took all the quizzes to see if I could make his fever rise (I always scored 100 percent), and even won first place in a Who's Rick Springfield's Favorite Fan essay contest. Rick was my first and only teen crush, coming into my life one month before my dad died unexpectedly. They say whatever happens to you right before a major tragedy forever gives you a feeling of comfort. Rick was that for me—then and through every decade since. College led me to California. And my career as a TV reporter took me to the lot where *General Hospital* was shot, though Dr. Noah Drake was long gone. Then, in the spring of 2000, something magical happened: The news desk called and asked me to work some overtime. Imagine my insane surprise when I learned it was the interview I'd been preparing for since the sixth grade. I almost fainted! And then a few years ago, for my 50th birthday party, I got the best present imaginable: *the* Rick Springfield, performing in person for me and my friends! I even got to sing along with him! I'm determined to have him over for a meal one of these days. Whatever menu I would choose, should this fantasy meal come true, I'd definitely start with this favorite salad of mine.

CREAMY POPPY SEED DRESSING

¾ cup mayonnaise (I use an avocado-based one)

¼ cup almond milk or milk of choice

¼ cup white wine vinegar or apple cider vinegar

2 tablespoons powdered sugar or 4 or 5 drops liquid stevia

1 tablespoon poppy seeds

½ teaspoon dry mustard

Salt and pepper, to taste

SALAD

One 8- to 10-ounce bag spring greens mix or baby spinach leaves (about 8 loosely packed cups)

1 cup sliced fresh strawberries

¼ cup toasted slivered almonds

¼ to ½ cup crumbled feta

½ cup thinly sliced red onions, optional

1. **MAKE THE DRESSING:** Whisk together the mayonnaise, milk, vinegar, sugar, poppy seeds, and mustard in a medium bowl. Season to taste with salt and pepper.
2. **MAKE THE SALAD:** Toss together the greens, strawberries, almonds, feta, and onions, if using, in a large bowl.
3. Add ½ cup of the dressing to the salad and toss. Taste and add more dressing, if desired. Store any leftover dressing in an airtight container in the refrigerator for up to 1 week.

Grilled Steak and Charred Vegetable Salad

with Blue Cheese and Coffee-Balsamic Vinaigrette

SERVES 4

This salad is what I call a fancy Leftover Makeover. It totally justifies throwing an extra steak on the grill to stretch into a fabulous—and economical—next-night feast that tastes like a party! It's the perfect vehicle for any leftover grilled steak. And if corn on the cob and grilled onions happen to be on the menu, even better! My Coffee-Balsamic Vinaigrette is made for pulling together bold, smoky flavors like these. As long as you've got the grill fired up, now's your chance to find out if grilled lettuce—which has been in vogue for some time, especially here in California—is as weird as it sounds. (Spoiler alert: It's not. The outer leaves get a little charred and crispy around the edges, taking on a slightly nutty, caramelized flavor, while the inner leaves stay tender.) I think you'll be surprised in the best way!

COFFEE-BALSAMIC VINAIGRETTE

- 6 tablespoons extra-virgin olive oil
- 2 tablespoons brewed coffee
- 1 tablespoon honey-Dijon mustard
- 1 tablespoon balsamic vinegar
- Salt and pepper, to taste

SALAD

- ½ to 1 pound boneless ribeye steak (or leftover Marinated and Grilled Steak, page 210)
- Montreal Steak Seasoning, Magic Seasoning (page 28), or salt and pepper
- 1 large red or yellow onion, sliced ½ inch thick
- 3 tablespoons avocado oil, divided
- 1 or 2 ears corn, husks removed (see Hacks: Shucking and Stripping Corn, page 97)
- Salt and pepper, to taste
- 3 romaine lettuce hearts
- 1 cup cherry tomatoes, halved
- 4 ounces crumbled blue cheese
- Avocado slices, optional
- Fresh basil leaves, optional

1. **MAKE THE VINAIGRETTE:** Place the oil, coffee, mustard, and vinegar in a small bowl and whisk to blend. (Or place all the ingredients in a small jar with a tight lid and shake until blended.) Season to taste with salt and pepper.
2. **MAKE THE SALAD:** Preheat the grill on medium-high heat (375°F to 450°F) for at least 5 minutes. Season the steak with Montreal Steak Seasoning.
3. Place the onion in a bowl and toss with about 1 tablespoon of the oil and a little of the seasoning. Then grill using a grill basket until slightly charred, 2 or 3 minutes per side. Set aside on a plate.
4. Set the shucked corn on the grill, brush the kernels with about 1 tablespoon of the oil, and season to taste with salt and pepper. Grill until the kernels are tender and slightly charred, turning occasionally, 10 to 12 minutes. Set aside on a plate and cut the kernels off the cob (see Hack: Shucking and Stripping Corn, page 97).
5. Meanwhile, add the steak to the grill and cook on each side for 5 to 7 minutes, or until an instant-read thermometer inserted in the thickest part registers 130°F for medium-rare. Transfer to a cutting board, let cool for 5 to 10 minutes, and then slice thinly against the grain.
6. While the steak cools, grill the romaine for some extra smokiness, if desired: Cut an inch or two off the top of the leaves and, leaving the roots intact, brush the exterior with a little oil. Grill, turning every 2 or 3 minutes, until charred to your liking, 6 to 8 minutes.

7. Tear off the lettuce leaves, or cut them into bite-size pieces, and arrange them on a platter. Top with the steak slices, grilled onion slices, corn kernels, cherry tomatoes, cheese, and avocado slices and basil leaves, if using. Drizzle with the vinaigrette.
8. Store any leftover dressing in an airtight container in the refrigerator for up to 2 weeks; bring to room temperature and shake well before using.

Tip

To clean grill grates, cut an onion in half and skewer it on a grilling fork. Then rub the cut side over the grates. Discard the onion. Your grates will be crud-free and seasoned to add extra flavor to whatever you're grilling!

Drive-Thru Cheeseburger Salad

SERVES 1

For some of us of a certain . . . ahem . . . age, the tongue-twisting lyrics of that 1970s-era McDonald's jingle—"two all-beef patties, special sauce, pickles, cheese, lettuce, onion on a sesame seed bun"—still pop into our heads whenever we catch sight of the golden arches. I turned this order into a high-protein, low-carb salad one day in the parking lot when all I had time for was the drive-thru. I tossed the bun, the ketchup packets, and the "secret sauce" (mayo, sweet pickle relish, and several unidentified spices) and replaced them with sauces that deliver double the flavor for a fraction of the carbs. The result, I have to say, was not only delicious but a lot less messy to eat! Ask for no bun or save it to use elsewhere along with the ketchup packet.

- 1 McDonald's Double Quarter Pounder with Cheese (with lettuce, tomatoes, pickles, and onion)
- 1 large drink cup
- Plastic knife and spoon or fork
- 1 packet McDonald's Spicy Buffalo Sauce
- 1 packet McDonald's Creamy Ranch Sauce

1. Unwrap your burger on your car's console or tray if you have one and toss or save the bun and the ketchup packet for later.
2. Cut up the burgers, tomatoes, pickles, and onion with your knife and tear up the lettuce. Place them in the cup.
3. Squeeze the buffalo sauce and ranch sauce into the cup, mix well with the spoon or fork, and eat!

Egg Roll Bowls

SERVES 4

This egg roll–inspired meal in a bowl is exactly like you're eating the inside of one! It gives you all the feels of the classic Chinese appetizer, with none of the deep-frying. And you won't be hungry an hour later! I like to have a batch of this on hand in the fridge to zap in the microwave for a quick low-carb lunch or dinner when the kids have scattered and Scooter is off on a business trip.

- 1 pound ground meat of choice or plant-based substitute
- 2 tablespoons soy sauce, tamari, or Teriyaki Sauce (page 29)
- 1 teaspoon garlic powder
- 1 teaspoon ground ginger
- Salt and pepper, to taste
- One 8-ounce bag coleslaw mix
- 2 tablespoons chopped scallions
- 1 or 2 tablespoons sesame seeds, optional

1. Place the meat in a large skillet over medium-high heat. Add the soy sauce, garlic powder, and ginger, and cook until browned, stirring occasionally to break up the meat, about 10 minutes. Season to taste with salt and pepper.
2. Stir in the slaw mix and continue to cook until soft, about 5 minutes, tasting again for seasoning and adding more salt and pepper if desired. Top with scallions and sesame seeds, if using.

Teriyaki Salmon and Cauliflower "Rice" Bowl

SERVES 1 OR 2

When I first saw the viral Salmon and Rice Bowl pop up on my feed, I made one of those "I'm not really sure about that" faces! Too many ingredients, too many steps, and definitely too many carbs for my liking . . . I just swiped out of it. Then it popped up again . . . then again, and so by the umpteenth time, I decided to tweak it just for fun. And my version is delicious, if I say so myself. If salmon isn't your thing, sub chicken, tuna, or tofu. The avocado will give you some healthy fat, and if your kids have a bag of seaweed snacks hanging around, try it with those as well. Chopped cucumber or thawed frozen edamame would also be good here.

- One 8.5-ounce bag microwavable riced cauliflower, cooked according to package directions
- One 5-ounce can wild salmon packed in water, drained, or leftover cooked salmon
- 1 scallion, chopped
- 1 tablespoon teriyaki sauce (see Teriyaki Sauce, page 29), plus more, as desired
- 1 avocado, peeled, seeded and cut into chunks (see Hack: The Best Way to Peel an Avocado and Turn It Into Guacamole, page 102)
- ½ cup chopped cucumber, optional
- ½ cup frozen shelled edamame, thawed, optional
- Savory Kale Chips (page 128), optional
- Crumbled seaweed snacks, optional
- 1 or 2 teaspoons sesame seeds or everything bagel seasoning blend

1. Mix the riced cauliflower, salmon, scallion, and 1 tablespoon of the teriyaki sauce in a medium bowl. (Divide into individual serving bowls if you're sharing, or wrap up half for tomorrow's lunch.)
2. Add the avocado. If desired, add the cucumber, edamame, kale chips, and seaweed snacks to the bowl, sprinkle with the sesame seeds, and serve.

Weekends, Holidays, and Special Occasions

CHAPTER 5

Lazy Weekend Breakfasts and Brunches

With all of our traveling and busy schedules, I rarely have time to throw a dinner party together. I find brunch more relaxing and manageable, whether we're having company or just enjoying a fleeting moment when we're all home together during the day! Most of the recipes in this chapter can easily be whipped up just in time for everyone to roll out of bed, and several are designed to be made ahead the night before. Here you'll find the makings for an easy Mother's Day, Father's Day, or Easter feast and a few weekend-only sweet treats best served with coffee or tea.

All-in-One Brunch Casserole

SERVES 4

I created this budget-friendly crowd-pleaser for Scooter one Father's Day, and it contains just about everything you see on a breakfast menu at a diner, except for biscuits and gravy. With this hack, you can make an entire brunch in one dish with ready-made French toast and hash browns straight from the freezer—no need to thaw! Hearty and savory with a touch of sweetness, it is as easy to clean up as it is to assemble.

- Nonstick cooking spray
- 8 large eggs
- 2 cups milk (any kind)
- ½ teaspoon Magic Seasoning (page 28) or a pinch of salt and pepper
- 6 slices frozen store-bought French toast
- 1 pound bacon, cooked until crisp and drained
- 1½ cups (about 12 ounces) frozen shredded hash browns
- 8 ounces cheddar, shredded (about 2 cups)

1. Preheat the oven to 350°F. Spray a 9 x 13-inch baking pan with cooking spray.
2. Beat together the eggs, milk, and Magic Seasoning in a large bowl until blended.
3. Line the bottom of the baking pan with the frozen French toast slices. Top with a layer of the bacon and then the frozen hash browns. Sprinkle evenly with the cheese and then pour the egg mixture over all the ingredients.
4. Bake for 30 to 45 minutes, until the eggs are set and the top is bubbly. Let rest for 5 minutes before serving.

Storage Tip

This casserole can be wrapped tightly with plastic wrap and a layer of foil after baking and refrigerated for up to 4 days, or frozen for up to 3 months.

To reheat: If frozen, thaw in the refrigerator overnight. Unwrap and then cover with a layer of parchment and foil to prevent overbrowning and place in a 350°F oven for 20 to 30 minutes, long enough to heat through.

German Puffy Pancake

SERVES 2 TO 4

Hands down, this is the recipe page with the most stains on it in my family cookbook! If you're going to make one thing out of this book, have it be this one. And make sure your family is standing around when you pull this puffy wonder out of the oven, as they just might start clapping. Oh, did I mention it's easy? No need to let your family know that part . . .

BATTER

⅔ cup all-purpose flour

⅔ cup milk or half-and-half

4 large or 5 medium eggs

1 tablespoon granulated sugar

½ teaspoon salt

2 tablespoons butter

LEMON SUGAR TOPPING

Juice of 1 lemon (see Hack: Juicing a Lemon, page 47)

¼ cup powdered sugar

CINNAMON SUGAR TOPPING

¼ cup granulated sugar

1 tablespoon ground cinnamon

Fresh fruit (choose your faves: sliced bananas, strawberries, peaches, blueberries, or citrus), for serving

1. Preheat the oven to 400°F. Place a large cast-iron skillet in the oven.
2. **MAKE THE BATTER:** Place the flour, milk, eggs, sugar, and salt in a bowl and whisk until combined, leaving it lumpy, if desired. (This can also be done in a blender.)
3. Carefully remove the pan from the oven and add the butter, swirling to melt. Pour in the batter.
4. Bake the pancake in the oven for 20 minutes, or until puffy and browned.
5. Here are two delicious options for garnishing your pancake. **LEMON SUGAR PANCAKE:** Squeeze the lemon juice over the hot pancake and immediately sift powdered sugar over top. **CINNAMON SUGAR PANCAKE:** Combine the sugar and cinnamon in a small bowl and sprinkle over the pancake. Serve immediately with fresh fruit.

Crescent Roll–Crusted Quiche

SERVES 6

Anything that calls for a crust outside of a pie for the holidays just makes my eyes glaze over! It's a daunting step I just don't have time for, especially on a weeknight. Enter one of the best things ever created: refrigerated crescent rolls. You will be shocked at how good they taste when turned into a pie crust. The texture is different for sure—it's softer and lighter, but IMO, it tastes even better! Once you try it, you may never go back.

- One 8-ounce can refrigerated Pillsbury Original Crescent Rolls
- 7 large eggs
- ½ cup heavy cream
- 1 cup shredded cheddar or Swiss cheese
- 4 to 6 slices cooked and chopped bacon or ½ cup chopped ham
- 1 teaspoon Magic Seasoning (page 28)
- Chopped chives, for garnish

1. Preheat the oven to 350°F. Unroll the crescent roll can and separate the rolls into eight triangles. Arrange the triangles on a 9-inch glass pie plate with the skinny tips in the center and the wider sections rolled out to the edge, covering the bottom and sides. Press down to create a crust in the pan, allowing enough overhang to make a nice border. Press the seams together and trim off any excess dough.
2. Bake for 10 minutes. Remove from the oven; let cool slightly.
3. Meanwhile, whisk the eggs and cream in a large bowl. Add the cheese, bacon, and Magic Seasoning, and mix well.
4. Pour the egg mixture into the partially baked crust and bake for about 45 minutes, or until the filling is set. Check periodically; if the crust starts to get too dark, cover the edges with foil. Let cool slightly before garnishing with chives and then slicing.

Love Bacon

MAKES 10 TO 12 SLICES

We call this "love bacon" at our house. It's sweet, savory, salty, and peppery all at once—what's not to love? And if the rogue splatter of frying bacon gives you grief, here's the best part: You can put away the skillet and simply turn on the oven instead. What could be easier? It's love on a platter.

- One 16-ounce package smoked, uncured thick-cut bacon slices (about 10 to 12 slices)
- ⅓ to ½ cup maple syrup
- ½ teaspoon freshly ground pepper

1. Preheat the oven to 400°F. Line a large baking sheet with parchment paper.
2. Lay your bacon slices on the parchment. Drizzle with maple syrup and grind pepper over them all.
3. Place in the oven and bake for 18 to 20 minutes, until the bacon is crispy but not burnt.

Storage Tip

Once cooled to room temperature, the quiche can be wrapped tightly with plastic wrap and a layer of foil and refrigerated for up to 3 days, or frozen for up to 3 months.

To reheat: If frozen, thaw in the refrigerator overnight. Unwrap and then cover with a layer of parchment and foil to prevent overbrowning and place in a 350°F oven for 15 to 20 minutes, long enough to heat through.

Ham and Cheese Bread Wreath

SERVES 4 TO 8

I love serving this at Easter with shredded lettuce and a few colored eggs. But it's also the perfect lunch dish for any time of year. Add chips to the middle for a tailgate or serve on a weeknight with a cup of tomato soup. I'm telling you: Ham and cheese just tastes better served this way! This wreath-making technique with dough can also be applied to other fillings, such as a Crescent Roll Taco Ring (see below).

Two 8-ounce cans refrigerated Pillsbury Original Crescent Rolls

2 cups shredded cheddar or Swiss cheese (8 ounces)

8 ounces shaved ham or other deli meat

FOR SERVING, OPTIONAL

Honey mustard dipping sauce

Deviled eggs or Easter eggs

1. Preheat the oven to 375°F. Line a large baking sheet with parchment paper.
2. Unroll both cans of dough and separate into 16 triangles. Arrange the triangles in a circle on the baking sheet so that the widest part of each triangle overlaps slightly and the opposite ends point outward, leaving a 5-inch hole in the center.
3. Sprinkle half the cheese on the widest half of each triangle. Top with the ham, followed by the remaining cheese.
4. Bring the opposite end of each triangle over the filling and tuck it under the bottom layer of dough to hold it in place.
5. Bake for 20 to 25 minutes, until golden brown and baked through. Let cool for 10 minutes and then transfer to a serving platter. If desired, put the honey mustard sauce in a small bowl and place it in the center for dipping, or serve it on the side and fill the center with deviled eggs or Easter eggs.

Crescent Roll Taco Ring

For a fun and festive presentation that's great for dinner, brunch, or a casual get-together, substitute Taco Bell–Style Seasoned Meat (see page 98) and Mexican blend shredded cheese for the ham and cheese. Bake at 375°F for 17 minutes, or until golden brown. Fill the center with chopped lettuce, diced tomato, sliced olives, and guacamole (kind of like a taco salad in the middle).

Four-Ingredient Blueberry Cinnamon Buckle

SERVES 6

Sweet mother of pearl! This coffee cake hack leaves me speechless . . . and you know that takes a lot! It's called a buckle, which refers to that old-time fruit-filled single-layer cake with a batter that "buckles" with its streusel topping as it bakes. But there's no batter or streusel to mess with here; a can of cinnamon roll dough saves you that step. You just cut the cinnamon rolls up in chunks, layer them with blueberries and brown sugar–sweetened cream cheese, and bake. The taste is like a cinnamon bun and bread pudding had a baby. Served warm straight from the oven, it's a surefire hit for brunch—and for that matter, any time of day or night! I use Pillsbury Grands! Cinnamon Rolls made with Cinnabon cinnamon and original icing for this recipe.

- Nonstick cooking spray
- One 17.5-ounce can refrigerated Pillsbury Grands! Cinnamon Rolls (5 count)
- 1 cup fresh or frozen blueberries
- One 8-ounce package cream cheese, softened
- ⅓ cup packed brown sugar

1. Preheat the oven to 375°F. Spray a 9-inch square baking pan with cooking spray.
2. Cut each roll into six chunks and spread them on the bottom of the prepared pan. Set the frosting packet aside. Sprinkle the blueberries on top.
3. Whisk the cream cheese and brown sugar in a medium bowl. Spread over the rolls and blueberries and gently stir to incorporate.
4. Bake for 30 to 40 minutes, until bubbly. Top with the frosting packet while warm.

Storage Tip

Once cooled to room temperature, this coffee cake can be wrapped in its pan (unfrosted), with plastic wrap and a layer of foil, and stored in the refrigerator for up to 3 days, or in the freezer for up to 3 months. If frozen, thaw in the refrigerator overnight. Unwrap and then cover with parchment and foil and place in a 350°F oven for 10 to 15 minutes, long enough to heat through. Top with the frosting packet while warm.

Flaky Chocolate Cheesecake Pastries

MAKES 12

These decadent treats look and taste like something you'd see at a French bakery! Crescent roll dough takes on a different shape here as it bakes up into crispy, petite bundles oozing with warm Nutella and gooey cream cheese. My favorite part: They're not only a crowd-pleaser on a brunch buffet, they're also the perfect size for a little sweet treat to go with your afternoon coffee or tea.

- ½ cup chocolate-hazelnut spread (such as Nutella)
- ½ cup (about ½ block) cream cheese, softened
- Three 4-count or one and a half 8-count cans refrigerated Pillsbury Original Crescent Rolls or Pillsbury Butter Flake Crescent Rolls
- Powdered sugar, for dusting

1. Preheat the oven to 375°F. Whip the chocolate spread and cream cheese in a medium bowl with an electric hand mixer on medium speed until thoroughly blended and fluffy, 2 or 3 minutes.
2. Unroll the dough from the cans and separate into triangles. Place the widest part of each triangle of dough into the bottom of a 12-cup muffin pan, allowing the ends of the pastry to hang over the top.
3. Place 1 tablespoon of the chocolate spread in the center of each cup and fold the ends of the pastry over the filling.
4. Bake for 15 to 20 minutes, until golden. Remove from the oven, let cool, and dust with powdered sugar.

Storage Tip

If you're not eating these pastries fresh out of the oven, it's best to freeze them the day you bake them to preserve their freshness. Once cooled to room temperature, wrap each one tightly in plastic wrap, place them in an airtight container or freezer-safe bag, and freeze for up to 3 months. To reheat, first let them thaw overnight in the refrigerator and then unwrap and rewarm in a 350°F oven for about 5 minutes.

Pumpkin Spice Donuts (or Muffins)

MAKES 14 TO 18

Kind of a cross between a muffin and a donut, these are shockingly good and moist—no oil or eggs required! A cinnamon sugar coating pairs perfectly with these, as would a drizzle of caramel, a smear of cream cheese frosting, or a simple dusting of powdered sugar. I use a gluten-free spice cake mix, but any flavor, even chocolate, will work. And they freeze beautifully! Don't have a donut pan? The batter is so thick that it can be piped into circles right onto a parchment-lined baking sheet. Or you can turn them into muffins by using a 12-cup muffin pan and adding a few minutes to the baking time.

- Nonstick cooking spray
- One 15.25-ounce box yellow or spice cake mix
- One 15-ounce can pure pumpkin
- ½ cup sugar
- 2 tablespoons ground cinnamon
- ½ cup (1 stick) melted butter, optional

1. Preheat the oven to 350°F. Spray three 6-cavity donut pans (3¼ inch in diameter) with cooking spray.
2. Mix the cake mix and pumpkin in a medium bowl with a large spoon or electric hand mixer. The batter will be thick. Scoop into a baggie, snip off the end, and squeeze into the prepared donut cavities. (Each should be no more than three-quarters full.)
3. Bake for 12 to 14 minutes, until the donuts start to brown and a cake tester inserted in the middle comes out clean.
4. Whisk the sugar and cinnamon in a small bowl.
5. Dip the donuts in the cinnamon sugar while warm so the mixture sticks. For a little more richness, you can also dip them first in melted butter and then in the cinnamon sugar mixture.

Storage Tip

Once cooled to room temperature, these donuts can be frozen with or without the cinnamon sugar coating. Place uncoated donuts in a single layer on a parchment-lined baking sheet and then freeze for about 3 hours, until solid (to keep them from sticking together). Transfer to an airtight container or freezer-safe bag. Wrap each coated donut individually in plastic wrap and then place them in a freezer-safe bag. Store in the freezer for up to 3 months.

To reheat: Thaw the frozen donuts on the counter until they reach room temperature and then place on a baking sheet and rewarm in an oven preheated to 300°F for 5 to 8 minutes. If uncoated, dip the warm donuts in the melted butter, if using, and the cinnamon sugar.

Three-Ingredient Ice Cream French Toast

SERVES 2 TO 4

I used to consider myself more of a pancake person than a French toast person until I discovered this crazy-easy hack. Nothing to crack, beat, or measure—the eggs, dairy, and flavorings are all there in a bowl of melted ice cream. Just dip, fry, and serve! Use any kind of bread and any flavor of ice cream. Brioche and French vanilla is always a winner, but how could you possibly go wrong with cinnamon swirl bread and butter pecan? You can make an entire loaf and freeze the leftovers or just make an individual serving. And if that's not fancy enough for you, top it off with a scoop of ice cream and your favorite sundae toppings.

1 pint ice cream (any flavor)
4 tablespoons (½ stick) butter, plus more for serving
4 thick slices brioche, challah, or other bread (stale works best)

FOR SERVING, OPTIONAL

Sliced bananas
Ice cream
Whipped cream
Nuts
Syrup

1. Dump the ice cream into a bowl and allow it to melt. (Or zap it in the microwave for about 15 seconds to speed up the process.)
2. Place the butter in a large skillet and allow it to melt over medium-low heat, swirling to coat the pan.
3. Dip a bread slice into the melted ice cream, add it to the pan, and fry, turning very carefully with a spatula or tongs (the wet bread can be delicate), until golden brown on both sides, 3 to 4 minutes per side. Transfer to a plate and repeat with the remaining slices.
4. Serve with more butter and other toppings as desired.

Fritos
The ORIGINAL

CHAPTER 6

Snacks and Apps for Sharing

When I was growing up in the Midwest, appetizers were pretty simple: It was almost always a crudité platter where you'd find pimento cheese, peanut butter, or both spread into celery stalks. So it won't be much of a surprise that Scooter and I aren't big on apps. That said, when the weekend rolls around, there are times that call for finger foods a few notches up from a bag of chips: the Super Bowl, family movie night, sleepovers, and cocktail (or mocktail) hour with the grown-ups. Rather than precursors to sit-down meals, these often become meals in themselves.

Fun with Cheese Crisps

Italians have been snacking on cheese crisps—aka frico—for centuries. And what's not to love? In their purest form, these addictive snacks consist of only one ingredient—cheese—that melts and hardens into crunchy discs on a griddle or in the oven. Delicious as they are, there are a million ways to get more creative with them by molding them in different shapes and pairing them with all kinds of goodies. Here are three of my favorites.

Cheddar Onion Rings

MAKES 12

I keep a simple donut pan handy for uses beyond making donuts, like these ring-shaped treats that satisfy my craving for onion rings without the extra carbs.

One 8-ounce package shredded cheddar or other cheese

1 small onion, sliced in rings as thick or thin as you like

Magic Seasoning (page 28)

1. Preheat the oven to 400°F. Distribute half the cheese evenly between the donut rings and lay the larger outer onion slices to fit the donut molds on top. (Save the inner slices for another use.)
2. Sprinkle lightly with Magic Seasoning and then cover with the remaining cheese. Bake for 10 to 15 minutes, until crispy.

Pizza Bites

MAKES 12

Say hello to my little friends: three ingredients, zero carbs, and they taste like pizza!

1½ cups shredded Italian blend cheese

1 tablespoon Italian seasoning

12 slices pepperoni (I use Applegate turkey pepperoni)

1. Preheat the oven to 375°F. Place 1 to 2 tablespoons cheese in each cup of a 12-cup muffin pan. Sprinkle each with a big pinch of Italian seasoning. Place one pepperoni slice on top of each.
2. Bake for 10 minutes, or until browned around the edges.

Tacos in a Cheese Cup

MAKES 8 TO 12

Mold mounds of melted cheese around the back of cupcake cups, and you have the perfect handheld low-carb container for taco meat or almost any savory filling.

Shredded Mexican blend cheese

Magic Seasoning (page 28), optional

Taco Bell–Styled Seasoned Meat (see page 98)

1. Line a baking sheet with parchment paper. Create piles of cheese (2 or 3 tablespoons each) about 2 inches apart. Sprinkle with Magic Seasoning, if desired.
2. Bake at 350°F for 5 to 7 minutes, until the edges are crispy. Remove from the oven and let rest for about 3 minutes.
3. Set a muffin pan upside down and place a cheese disc over the back of each cup. Press gently to form a mold and let cool.
4. Remove, turn right side up, and fill with Taco Bell–Style Seasoned Meat (see page 98) and toppings.

Easy Homemade Nacho Cheese

MAKES ABOUT 1¾ CUPS

You know I'm all for shortcuts, but since I've discovered how easy it is to make nacho cheese dip (or queso, as you might say), I may never go back to the jarred stuff again. The taste is vastly superior! It's great as a sauce to pour over tacos, or even vegetables, and as a dip with chips it's guaranteed to be the hit of any party. Serve as is or dress it up with salsa and some warmed leftover Taco Bell–Style Seasoned Meat (page 98).

One 8-ounce block mild cheddar, shredded
1½ teaspoons cornstarch
1½ cups half-and-half
1 teaspoon hot sauce, or to taste
¼ teaspoon cayenne pepper or taco seasoning, or to taste
¼ teaspoon salt, or to taste

ADD-INS, OPTIONAL

½ to 1 cup salsa, Ro-Tel tomatoes, or chopped fresh tomatoes
½ to 1 cup Taco Bell–Style Seasoned Meat (see page 98)

FOR SERVING

Tortilla chips
Raw veggies

1. Toss the cheese with the cornstarch in a medium bowl and set aside.
2. Pour the half-and-half into a medium saucepan and bring to a simmer over medium heat. Slowly add the cheese mixture, whisking constantly, until smooth.
3. Add the hot sauce, cayenne, and salt, and adjust to taste. Stir in or top with optional additions, if you like. Serve warm, with chips and/or raw veggies.

Storage Tip

After the dip cools to room temperature, transfer to an airtight container and refrigerate for up to 5 days. Reheat in a saucepan over low heat, stirring constantly, or in a microwave-safe dish in 30-second increments in the microwave, stirring after each interval to prevent burning.

Debi's Hot and Cheesy Onion Dip

MAKES ABOUT 6 CUPS

Out of my six sisters, two are "The Twins": Sandi and Debi. It's almost like you can't say one without the other. When I started talking to my family about their favorite dishes to put in a cookbook, Sandi was so adamant about this recipe making the cut that she texted me the next day with a picture of it to save me from flipping through the family cookbook to find it. Here's the sweet part: It's a dish Debi is actually known for making, not Sandi. Normally, that wouldn't be a big deal, but during the course of writing this book, we suddenly lost Sandi. At our large family gathering at my sister Kay's the night before Sandi's memorial, Debi brought this dish because Sandi would have most definitely requested it. Sandi loved it that much, and I hope you do, too.

12 to 16 ounces frozen chopped onions or 4 medium yellow or sweet onions, chopped

Three 8-ounce packages cream cheese, softened

2 cups grated Parmesan

½ cup mayonnaise

FOR SERVING

Corn chips

Assorted crackers

Raw veggies

1. Preheat the oven to 425°F. If you're using frozen onions, thaw them and roll in paper towels or a clean tea towel, squeezing to remove excess moisture.
2. Place the onions, cream cheese, Parmesan, and mayonnaise in a large bowl. Mix with a wooden spoon until well combined. Transfer to a shallow 2-quart soufflé dish or similar-sized pan.
3. Bake for about 30 to 40 minutes, until the dip is golden brown. Serve with corn chips, assorted crackers, and/or raw veggies for dipping.

Praline-Topped Brie "Flower"
with Breadstick Twists

SERVES 6

I will never forget the first time I had this eye-catching app, and neither will you. The nutty, buttery, caramelized topping you drag the hot bread pieces through to unveil the melted brie underneath will stick with you forever! I know it sounds dramatic, but it's just that good. And it makes such a pretty presentation. You simply twist the prepared breadstick dough, loop the twists around the brown sugar and pecan–topped brie so that it resembles a flower, and serve it in the glass pie plate you make it in. Only one dish to wash! Mark my words: It's the appetizer that will disappear first.

- One 5- or 6-inch brie wheel
- One 11-ounce can Pillsbury Original Breadsticks
- ½ cup brown sugar
- ½ cup chopped pecans or walnuts

1. Preheat the oven to 375°F. Skim the rind off the top of the brie with a sharp knife and discard. Place the brie wheel in the center of a 9-inch pie plate.
2. Unroll the breadstick dough. Twist each piece of dough and place around the brie. This should fill the pie plate and look like a flower.
3. Sprinkle the top of the brie with the brown sugar to completely cover the wheel and then sprinkle with the pecans. Bake for 14 to 16 minutes, until the breadsticks are golden brown and the brie has melted.
4. Serve warm and invite everyone to tear off a breadstick and dip it into the praline-topped melted cheese.

Hot Deviled Butter Dipping Sauce
for Crab and Other Seafood

MAKES ABOUT 1¾ CUPS

My mother-in-law, Gracie, God rest her soul, wasn't a cook, and she'd be the first to tell you that. In fact, when Scooter went off to college and all the other kids were talking about the food they missed from home, he realized he was the only one who couldn't think of a thing! But she did have a couple of simple recipes she had written on Post-its, and this is one of them. She made this dipping sauce for dunking crab claws and legs—an impressive, shareable party dish with practically no danger of failure. But really, it works on any kind of seafood. You could even just dip bread in this. (Adding breadsticks to your presentation is a great way to stretch your seafood splurge.) I strongly advise making a double batch so you don't run out when folks start drinking it!

- ¾ cup (1½ sticks) butter
- 2 tablespoons chili sauce
- 4 teaspoons lemon or lime juice
- 2 teaspoons yellow mustard
- 2 teaspoons Worcestershire sauce
- 2 or 3 drops Tabasco or other hot sauce
- 1 tablespoon finely chopped fresh parsley
- King or snow crab legs and claws or other seafood (1 to 2 pounds per person), cooked
- Breadsticks, optional

1. Place the butter, chili sauce, lemon juice, mustard, and Worcestershire sauce in a small saucepan. Bring the mixture to a simmer over medium heat, stirring to blend. Season with the hot sauce.
2. Stir in the parsley and serve warm, with seafood for dipping, along with breadsticks, if using.

Game Day Chicken Wing Cupcakes
with Hot Honey "Frosting"

MAKES ABOUT 18

I love a good chicken wing. Who doesn't? But I don't love going to the trouble of making them when I'm strapped for time and don't feel guilty a bit about buying them ready-made for a party! Whether your wings are store-bought or homemade, here's a fun way to make them soar to new heights. And with these guys, you don't have to wait for dessert! Here's the best part: You can use the cornbread cupcake like a little sponge for all the juicy goodness dripping from the chicken wing!

- Two 8-ounce packages cream cheese
- ¼ cup hot honey (or regular honey with 5 to 8 drops Tabasco or other hot sauce, to taste)
- 1 batch (about 18) Copycat Marie Callender's Cornbread Muffins (page 143)
- About 18 buffalo-style chicken wings

1. Place the cream cheese and honey in a medium bowl and beat with an electric hand mixer on medium speed until fluffy.
2. Spread a dollop of the frosting on each cupcake and top with a warm chicken wing. Serve immediately.

Mini Cinnamon Donut Cheeseburgers

MAKES 16

This wacky-sounding recipe is my take on the Luther Burger, one of my favorite food discoveries I tried some years ago at the Apple Fritter, a hip breakfast and lunch spot in the San Francisco Bay Area. On their menu, it consists of a ground beef patty topped with bacon, cheese, and a sunny-side up egg sandwiched between halves of a glazed donut. Actually, there are many riffs on this combo (supposedly a favorite of the singer-songwriter Luther Vandross) all over the country. And if you're from Kansas like me, where cinnamon rolls with chili is a thing (sometimes called "bowl and a roll"—I'm not kidding!), this would make perfect sense. I've combined both those ideas and scaled it down to a savory-sweet handheld treat, using my cute little donut machine. If you don't have one, you can just make mini cinnamon buns and burgers, and you'll get the same effect.

- One 12.4-ounce can refrigerated Pillsbury Cinnamon Rolls (8 count)
- 1 pound ground beef or other meat or meat alternative
- Magic Seasoning (page 28)
- 8 slices American cheese or cheese of choice, cut in half

1. Heat your mini donut maker as directed. Remove the cinnamon roll dough from the tube and set the frosting packet aside. Cut each cinnamon roll dough piece in half, roll into thin strips, and connect the ends, making a circle to fit the donut mold.
2. Place the dough circles in the donut maker and "bake" for about 2 minutes, or until golden brown (each machine is different, so check at about 1½ minutes in; you don't want to overbake them). Remove and set aside. Repeat until all the dough circles are baked. Slice each "donut" in half horizontally to make buns.
3. Divide the meat into 16 balls. Poke a hole in each one using the handle of a wooden spoon. Sprinkle generously with Magic Seasoning.
4. Place the meatballs in the donut machine and cook for about 2 minutes, or until cooked through. Remove the "burgers" from the donut machine. Repeat until all the burgers are cooked. Drain or wipe grease with a paper towel in between burgers as needed.
5. Place a burger on the bottom half of each donut. Top with a piece of cheese cut to fit, add the top half of the donut, and drizzle with the frosting packet, if desired.

Firecracker Popcorn

MAKES 2 HEAPING QUARTS

Popcorn, Pop Rocks, and chocolate: Separately they're delicious; together they are out of this world! My kids love popcorn and have come up with some pretty crazy combinations. Kid 2 does this thing where she coats hers in olive oil and salt and then dips it in yellow mustard! (It's surprisingly good.) Deciding to try this combo on the heels of that creation didn't sound so crazy. Pop Rocks, aka popping candy, are one of my favorite childhood candies. If you haven't had them yet, they're a type of hard candy that crackles as they dissolve in your mouth—making them the perfect match for popcorn and addition to any celebration that calls for fireworks! To enhance the color and flavor explosion, I throw in some mini M&M's as well.

- 2 quarts popped popcorn (from ⅓ cup kernels)
- Salt (popcorn salt or fine sea salt works best), to taste
- One extra-large (4.4-ounce) Hershey bar, or chocolate bar of choice, in a plastic wrapper
- One 9.4-ounce bag M&M's minis
- One 0.33-ounce packet Pop Rocks candy (or several, in assorted flavors and colors)

Watch me make this!

1. Spread the popped popcorn on a parchment-lined baking sheet and sprinkle lightly with salt.
2. Next up is my satisfying hack for melting chocolate, and it's going to blow you away! Bring a pot of water to a simmer and dip the wrapped bar into the pot. Wait a few seconds and then pull it out immediately. (The chocolate will melt fast, so make sure you don't walk away!)
3. Snip off a corner of the wrapper for a mess-free process and then squeeze over the kernels while the chocolate is hot. Sprinkle in the M&M's.
4. Now, here come the fireworks! Sprinkle the Pop Rocks over the kernels while the chocolate is warm. Then dig in!

TASTE THE

Veggie Ranch Pizza Squares

MAKES 32 APPETIZERS OR SERVES 6 TO 12 AS A LIGHT SNACK OR MEAL

In the 1970s, these were considered the "veggie pizzas" of my childhood. Easy to make, easy to take, and everyone loves 'em! In fact, this is a great way to get kids who wouldn't touch a veggie platter to eat an appetizer other than the chips. And zero chance of the little munchkins double-dipping in the ranch. If you want to get an early start, cover the cooled crust with plastic wrap and let it stand at room temperature before adding the toppings. You can cover and refrigerate it for up to 2 hours before serving, but don't push it—too long and the crust could get soggy.

Two 8-ounce cans refrigerated Pillsbury Original Crescent Rolls or Pillsbury Original Crescent Dough Sheets

One 8-ounce package cream cheese, softened (see Note)

½ cup sour cream

1 to 2 tablespoons ranch seasoning mix

FOR SERVING, OPTIONAL

Torn fresh basil leaves

Small broccoli florets

Shredded carrots

Chopped chives

Sliced cucumbers

Sliced olives

Diced bell peppers

Sliced scallions or red onions

Halved cherry tomatoes

1. Preheat the oven to 375°F. Unroll both cans of the crescent rolls and separate the dough into four long rectangles. Press in the bottom and up the sides of an ungreased 15 x 10 x 1-inch or 13 x 9 x 1-inch baking pan to form the crust. (Or unroll both cans of dough sheets and press into the pan.)
2. Bake for 13 to 17 minutes, until golden brown. Remove from the oven and allow the crust to cool completely, about 30 minutes.
3. Meanwhile, mix the cream cheese, sour cream, and ranch seasoning in a medium bowl with a wooden spoon or an electric hand mixer on medium speed until the mixture is smooth and well blended. (Start with 1 tablespoon seasoning and add more to taste, as it is quite salty.)
4. Spread the mixture over the cooled crust and arrange your preferred veggies decoratively over the top. Serve immediately, or cover and chill for up to 2 hours (no longer or the crust will start to turn soggy).

Note

If the cream cheese is still too hard to blend, unwrap it and set it on a microwave-safe plate and zap it in the microwave on high for 15 to 20 seconds.

CHAPTER 7

Stress-Free Sunday and Holiday Feasts

As the youngest of nine kids, I was used to taking part in huge feasts. Over the years, I've learned to modify the prep for those festivities significantly, whether we're talking about a routine Sunday supper or our annual Thanksgiving blowout. Most often, I'll focus on one large roast or other hunk of meat and prepare it simply, with a game plan for using up leftovers creatively. This chapter focuses on the meaty centerpieces for those events that can generate fabulous leftovers, plus hefty make-ahead casseroles, festive salads and sides, and simple, economical ways to stretch the extras. Make one of these meals on Sunday and skip worrying about dinner on Monday!

HACK: DIY Roasting Pan

For even browning, it's important to keep your bird raised while it roasts. But if you don't have a roasting pan with a rack, there's no need to go out and buy one! Try this hack instead: Line a roasting pan, large baking pan, or baking sheet with raised sides with parchment and set a heavy-duty wire rack on top. Spray with nonstick cooking spray, set your turkey on top of the rack, and you're good to go.

No-Baste Thanksgiving Turkey
with Photogenic Dressing

SERVES 12 TO 20 (WITHOUT LEFTOVERS) OR 8 TO 14 (WITH LEFTOVERS)

I'm from a huge family of foodies whose motto for family gatherings could be that old Burger King jingle: "Have it your way." At Thanksgiving, lines have been drawn so deep in the sand that we make three turkeys: one deep-fried, one smoked, and one roasted. Since deep-frying isn't for me and smoking can be daunting, I needed a good old-fashioned work-around that anyone could do. This turkey requires no special tools—all you need is a piece of cheesecloth and things you've already got hanging out in your kitchen. This is easy, and the payoff is huge! My method of swaddling turkey in butter-soaked cheesecloth before roasting is one of my most popular videos and gives new meaning to turkey dressing! No more setting a timer to baste the turkey every half hour and stressing about it drying out. It comes out moist, browned, and perfect every time.

- One 12- to 20-pound turkey, thawed if frozen
- ½ cup (1 stick) butter, room temperature, plus 1 cup (2 sticks), melted
- Salt and pepper
- 1 medium orange, quartered
- 1 small onion, quartered
- 1 celery stalk, chopped
- 2 or 3 fresh rosemary sprigs
- 2 or 3 fresh thyme sprigs
- ½ medium apple
- Kitchen string
- 1 large piece of cheesecloth

1. Remove the top and middle racks of the oven, only leaving the lowest rack. Preheat the oven to 350°F. Remove the turkey from the bag. Remove the bag of giblets and set aside to use in other recipes, if desired. Remove any excess fat and pat the outside of the turkey dry with paper towels.
2. Place on a roasting pan or make your own (see Hack).
3. Rub the turkey with the room-temperature butter outside, inside, and under the skin. Season the turkey with salt and pepper outside and inside the cavity.
4. Fill the cavity with the orange, onion, celery, rosemary, and thyme. Cork the cavity opening with the apple. Tie the legs together with kitchen string and tuck the wings under the body.
5. Place the melted butter in a large container with the cheesecloth. Drape the butter-soaked cheesecloth over the turkey, completely covering it.
6. Place in the oven and set the timer for 13 minutes per pound (about 2½ hours for a 12-pound turkey and 4 hours for a 20-pounder). Resist the urge to peek—just let the magic happen.
7. When the timer goes off, insert an instant-read thermometer in the meatiest part of the thigh. If it registers between 160°F and 165°F, it's done. (Alternatively, you can check by cutting between the thigh and the leg with a sharp knife to see if the juices run clear.) If it's not quite done, return it to the oven for 5 more minutes or so and check again.
8. Allow the turkey to rest for at least 20 minutes, but no more than 2 hours, before slicing and serving.
9. While the turkey roasts, prepare the Photogenic Turkey Dressing (page 206) and bake in the 350°F oven while the turkey rests. Transfer the turkey to a platter and reserve the drippings for Mom's Gravy (page 209).

Photogenic Turkey Dressing

SERVES UP TO 12

Raise your hand if you agree with the following statement: Stuffing (dressing) is one of the most unattractive holiday dishes out there! It's one of the best-tasting and worst-looking foods at the same time. Here's how to make this brown wonder the star of not only your plate but also the entire buffet. This photogenic dressing has more crunchy surfaces than your average dressing, so there's less fighting for those edges! These days I have no shame in taking the shortcut with a boxed mix (my favorites are Trader Joe's Cornbread Stuffing and Mrs. Cubbison's Traditional Seasoned Stuffing). But in the unlikely event I choose to go purist, I'll sub in equal parts dried sourdough and cornbread cubes, 2 tablespoons of dry rubbed sage, and 1 teaspoon salt.

- Nonstick cooking spray
- 8 cups seasoned dry stuffing mix
- 4 tablespoons (½ stick) butter
- 2 cups chopped celery
- 2 cups chopped onion (about 2 medium onions)
- 32 ounces chicken broth
- 4 large eggs, beaten
- Cranberry Sauce (see below), for serving, optional

1. Preheat the oven to 350°F. Spray a Bundt pan with nonstick cooking spray. Combine the stuffing mix with the packet seasonings in a large bowl.
2. Melt the butter in a large skillet over medium heat. Add the celery and onion and cook, stirring, until very tender, 5 to 7 minutes. Pour the butter and veggie mixture over the bread cubes. Add 3½ cups of the broth and the eggs and mix well. Add more broth if the mixture seems too dry.
3. Pour the mixture into the prepared Bundt pan and bake for 50 to 60 minutes, until set and crispy around the edges. Let cool slightly, 10 minutes or so and then loosen the edges with a thin silicone or plastic knife and flip over onto a large platter so that the rounded side with the pretty ridges is on top. If desired, to make it even more photogenic, place a small bowl in the hole in the center of the mold and fill it with the cranberry sauce. Or just pour the sauce directly into the center.

Cranberry Sauce

MAKES 2¾ CUPS

It wouldn't be Thanksgiving without the classic crimson condiment, made according to the formula that simply can't be improved upon no matter how much you try to mess with it.

- 1 cup water
- ½ to 1 cup sugar (depending on your desired sweetness)
- One 12-ounce bag fresh cranberries
- Zest and juice of 1 orange, optional

1. Bring the water and sugar to a boil in a medium saucepan over medium heat. Add the cranberries and cook until they start to split, about 10 minutes. You can smash them a little or leave them whole.
2. Add the orange zest and juice, if using. Turn off the heat and let the sauce cool to room temperature. The sauce will thicken as it cools. Transfer to a container, cover with a lid, and refrigerate for up to 2 weeks.

Mom's Gravy

MAKES 1½ TO 2 CUPS

If you want to go with gravy from the can or a mix, I won't judge! But really, it's easy to make from scratch if you do it the way my mom taught me, starting with my No-Baste Thanksgiving Turkey (page 205).

1. Place 1 cup cold water and ¼ cup flour in a jar and screw the lid on. Shake well until the mixture is thoroughly blended with no lumps. (You can also whisk the two together in a bowl.)
2. After you've removed the turkey from the roasting pan, heat the remaining drippings in the pan over medium heat and slowly add the flour mixture, whisking as you bring it to a boil. Continue to whisk until bubbly, adding more water or broth (if you have it) if it's too thick.
3. Transfer to a gravy boat and serve.

Leftover Turkey Dinner Bites

MAKES AS MANY AS YOU CAN ASSEMBLE BEFORE YOUR LEFTOVERS RUN OUT!

I came up with this hack a few years ago when I got tired of pulling out all of the leftovers from the fridge to create a little snack. So I decided to turn them into savory whole-meal muffins, to keep the turkey from drying out. It's a tidy way to streamline your fridge while supplying you with extras to last you into the New Year. Serve with cranberry sauce, if you've got it.

- Leftover bread or cornbread dressing, from Photogenic Turkey Dressing (page 206)
- Cooked turkey slices, from No-Baste Thanksgiving Turkey (page 205)
- Mashed potatoes or sweet potatoes (or both!)
- Mom's Gravy (see above)

1. Line a 12-cup muffin pan with cupcake liners and fill them about one-third full with the leftover dressing. Add turkey slices and then spread them with mashed potatoes to within about ¼ inch of the top.
2. "Frost" each with some of the gravy. This will help keep everything from drying out when you reheat it.
3. Cover the top with two layers of parchment for extra protection, wrap tightly in plastic wrap, and pop the pan into the freezer until the turkey bites are frozen.
4. Pop the bites out of the pan and place in freezer bags until ready to use.
5. To reheat, remove the cupcake liner and place the turkey bite on a microwave-safe plate. Set it at the edge of the plate inside the microwave for even heating, and microwave on high for 1 or 2 minutes, until hot.

More Leftover Tips

Swap in turkey for chicken in any of these recipes: Waldorf-Inspired Chicken Salad (page 149); Chicken, Grapefruit, and Butter Lettuce Salad à la Amy's (page 150); No-Lift White Chicken or Turkey Chili (page 106); or Weeknight Croque Monsieurs (page 93).

Marinated and Grilled Steak

with Chimichurri Sauce

SERVES 4 TO 6

When meat prices skyrocket, it's hard to justify splurging on a T-bone or ribeye. Treat yourself to a steak dinner for less by cooking a flank or skirt steak instead. Both are quite lean and have a deep, beefy flavor, with long, tough fibers that can give those molars quite a workout if you don't give the meat a little extra TLC. A good soak in a tenderizing bath of acid, oil, and salt before grilling solves this problem while infusing it with extra flavor. Slicing it thinly across the grain for serving makes it easier to chew, too. It's delicious served simply with a drizzle of some of the pungent leftover marinade (brought to a boil first to avoid contamination) but even better slathered in chimichurri sauce as they do in the best Argentinian steak houses—and in our backyard!

- 1 teaspoon Magic Seasoning (page 28) or ½ teaspoon salt and ¼ teaspoon each pepper and garlic powder
- 2 to 3 pounds flank or skirt steak (see Note)
- ⅔ cup balsamic vinegar
- ¼ cup avocado oil
- ¼ cup tamari or soy sauce
- ¼ cup Worcestershire sauce, optional
- 1 teaspoon minced garlic, optional
- 2 batches Creamy Chimichurri Sauce (page 28), optional

1. Sprinkle the Magic Seasoning evenly over all sides of the steak and place it in a large zip-top bag.
2. Add the vinegar, oil, tamari, and Worcestershire sauce and garlic, if using, to the bag and shake it around to coat. Place the steak in the refrigerator to marinate for as little as 15 minutes (for a thin ½-inch skirt steak) and up to 24 hours (for a thick 1-inch or more flank steak), flipping the steak halfway through.
3. Remove the steak from the refrigerator 30 to 60 minutes before grilling, if time permits, to bring it closer to room temperature. (If you can't, don't stress about it—it will still taste great.)
4. Heat an outdoor grill or indoor grill pan to medium-high (450°F when the lid of the outdoor grill is closed).
5. Remove the steak from the marinade and grill for 3 to 8 minutes on each side (depending on thickness), until an instant-read thermometer inserted in the thickest part reaches 130°F to 140°F for medium-rare (or 145°F for medium). Transfer the steak to a cutting board, cover with a piece of parchment and foil, and let rest for 10 to 15 minutes to allow the juices to settle in.
6. Thinly slice the meat across the grain on the diagonal. Serve with Creamy Chimichurri Sauce, if using. Or bring the leftover marinade to a boil in a small saucepan (to kill any harmful bacteria) and drizzle over the meat.

Leftover Tip

Stretch any extra steak into a whole-meal salad, such as the Grilled Steak and Charred Vegetable Salad with Blue Cheese and Coffee-Balsamic Vinaigrette (page 154).

Note

This marinade also works well with chicken and tofu. Don't leave them in the marinade too long, though—30 minutes tops.

Mississippi Mud Roast

SERVES 6 TO 8

This is one of those recipes that has made the rounds for years. I think I first picked it up in a newspaper article that one of my friends had copied and emailed around. I grew up eating pot roast almost every Sunday night, but my family's way of making it requires dipping in flour, searing in butter, slicing divots in the roast, and pushing garlic cloves in the meat . . . you get the idea; it's just a lot of work. So when I found this, it quickly replaced the one we've been handwriting and passing down for decades. It's tender, rich, savory, and tingly in all the right ways! Sorry Mom and Tre, I know where you stand on the searing, but trust me, you don't "Mississippi" that step with this one.

- One 3- to 5-pound chuck roast
- One 1-ounce packet ranch seasoning mix
- One 0.87-ounce packet brown gravy mix or au jus gravy mix
- 5 or 6 bottled pepperoncini
- ½ cup (1 stick) butter
- ¼ cup pepperoncini brine from the bottle, optional
- Mashed potatoes, cooked pasta, or cooked rice, for serving

1. Place the chuck roast in a large slow cooker, empty the packets of ranch seasoning mix and gravy mix on top, and add the pepperoncini and butter. Cover and cook on low for 8 to 10 hours, until the meat is fork-tender.
2. Shred the meat and drizzle with some of the pepperoncini brine for extra spice, if using. Serve over mashed potatoes, pasta, or rice.

Leftover Tip

Serve leftover pot roast and gravy over hot, open-faced Butter Swim Biscuits (page 144).

Slow-Cooker Pork Loin
with Apples and Onions

SERVES 6 TO 8

Pork and apples is a classic winning flavor combo. For many of us growing up, that meant applesauce served alongside pork chops. This recipe elevates that idea, using a whole pork loin, fresh apples, and additional layers of flavor provided by onions, honey, balsamic vinegar, and a few basic seasonings. There's no searing required here—just throw everything in the slow cooker and remember to check the internal temperature with an instant-read thermometer on the early side so it stays nice and moist.

1 onion, thinly sliced
2 green apples, thinly sliced
½ cup (1 stick) butter, sliced into pats
One 2½- to 3-pound boneless pork loin
2 teaspoons Magic Seasoning (page 28)
¼ teaspoon ground cinnamon
¼ teaspoon dried thyme
¼ cup honey
¼ cup balsamic vinegar
Finely chopped fresh thyme, optional

1. In your slow cooker, layer the ingredients in this order, starting from the bottom: onions, apples, butter pats, pork, Magic Seasoning, cinnamon, dried thyme, honey, and vinegar.
2. Cook on low for 3 to 4 hours, until the middle of the pork loin registers 155°F on an instant-read thermometer. (Be careful not to overcook so the meat doesn't dry out.)
3. Slice the pork loin and serve with the onions and apples. Garnish with fresh thyme, if using.

Leftover Tip

Turn a baked sweet potato (see Hack: Shortcut Baked Potato, page 132) into a whole meal by stuffing it with the leftover pork, apples, and onions. If you like, sprinkle the top with some grated cheddar or goat cheese and pop it in a 350°F oven for 5 to 10 minutes, until hot and bubbly.

The Ultimate Sweet Potato Casserole

SERVES 8 TO 10

Sweet potato casserole has been my contribution to every holiday meal for as long as I've been cooking, and I tinkered with my recipe for years before I finally nailed it. I have yet to take this somewhere without being asked for the recipe. I also love it because I can make it well ahead of time and freeze it. The marshmallow topping is optional in my book, but the nuts are essential—in both the potato mixture and the topping. I also like to throw in bits of pineapple for a tropical twist.

SWEET POTATO LAYER

- Nonstick cooking spray or softened butter, for greasing
- Three 15-ounce cans sweet potatoes
- ¼ cup packed brown sugar
- ¼ to ½ cup half-and-half or heavy cream
- 2 large eggs, lightly beaten
- 3 tablespoons salted butter, melted
- 1½ teaspoons ground cinnamon
- 1 teaspoon vanilla extract
- ½ teaspoon salt
- ¼ teaspoon ground allspice
- ¼ teaspoon ground nutmeg, preferably freshly ground
- ½ cup chopped pecans
- ½ cup fresh and chopped or canned and drained pineapple

TOPPING

- 1 cup chopped pecans
- ½ cup packed brown sugar
- ⅓ cup (⅔ stick) salted butter, melted
- ⅓ cup all-purpose flour
- 2 cups mini marshmallows, optional

1. Preheat the oven to 350°F. Coat the bottom of a 9 x 13-inch baking pan with nonstick cooking spray.
2. **MAKE THE SWEET POTATO LAYER:** Place the sweet potatoes in a large bowl and mash with a potato masher until smooth (some chunks won't hurt). Add the brown sugar, half-and-half, eggs, butter, cinnamon, vanilla, salt, allspice, and nutmeg, and stir with a wooden spoon until well blended. (You can also mix the ingredients in a food processor fitted with a steel blade or with an electric hand mixer, but take care not to overprocess.)
3. Stir in the pecans and pineapple and then pour the mixture into the prepared pan.
4. **MAKE THE TOPPING:** Mix the pecans, brown sugar, butter, and flour in a medium bowl until well combined. Sprinkle evenly on top of the sweet potato layer. Bake for 35 to 45 minutes, until the sides begin to bubble.
5. If topping with marshmallows, remove the pan from the oven after baking and pour the marshmallows over the top. Return the pan to the oven for 5 more minutes, or until the marshmallows are golden brown and puffy.

Storage Tip

To refrigerate or freeze: Cool the casserole, cover tightly with plastic wrap, and refrigerate for up to 4 days, or freeze (without the marshmallows) for up to 3 months.

To reheat: If frozen, thaw in the refrigerator overnight. Remove the plastic wrap and cover with parchment and foil. Place in a 350°F oven for 20 to 30 minutes, until heated through. Remove the foil and parchment and return to the oven for an additional 5 minutes or so (with marshmallows added, if you wish) to get the top nice and toasty.

Tater Tot Casserole

SERVES 10 TO 12

As if tater tots aren't good enough on their own! This rich, cheesy casserole takes them to the next level. This community cookbook staple is a favorite at our house and a comforting crowd-pleaser that's super easy to whip up. It's an instant hit on any buffet table and can be served as a side dish or main with a salad. And best of all, it can be made ahead, frozen, and popped in the oven directly from the freezer. The leftovers taste great for days.

- Softened butter or nonstick cooking spray, for greasing
- One 1¾-pound bag frozen tater tots
- 4 cups shredded cheddar, divided
- One 10.5-ounce can cream of mushroom or cream of chicken soup
- 2 cups sour cream
- 1 cup (2 sticks) melted butter, divided
- 1 cup finely chopped onion (about ½ large onion)
- 2 teaspoons Magic Seasoning (page 28)
- 2 cups crushed cornflakes
- Chopped fresh chives or parsley, optional

1. Preheat the oven to 350°F. Coat the bottom of a 9 x 13-inch baking pan with softened butter.
2. Combine the tater tots, 2 cups of the cheese, the soup, the sour cream, ½ cup of the melted butter, the onion, and then Magic Seasoning in a large bowl. Mix well and then pour the mixture into the prepared pan. Sprinkle the remaining 2 cups cheese on top.
3. Mix the cornflakes and the remaining ½ cup butter in a medium bowl and stir to coat. Spread the mixture in an even layer on top of the cheese.
4. Transfer to the oven and bake, uncovered, for 45 minutes, or until bubbly and browned on top. Garnish with the chives before serving, if using.

Storage Tip

To refrigerate or freeze: Cool the casserole, cover tightly with plastic wrap, and refrigerate for up to 4 days, or freeze for up to 3 months.

To reheat: If frozen, first let it thaw in the refrigerator overnight, or until completely thawed. Remove the plastic wrap and then cover with parchment and foil to prevent it from drying out. Place in a 350°F oven for 30 to 40 minutes, until heated through. Remove the foil and parchment and return to the oven for 5 or 10 minutes to crisp up the top.

Cheese Grits Soufflé

SERVES 6 TO 8

Southerners like to eat grits with eggs for breakfast, but at our house, it's welcome at any meal, especially this way! This cheesy casserole that puffs up a little like a soufflé is Scooter's favorite. It would be especially good with the Slow-Cooker Pork Loin with Apples and Onions (page 214) or as a side at any big holiday dinner. I usually make one large serving, but making this in individual ramekins gives it a fancy feel. It also happens to freeze well, even if it's no longer fluffy.

- Softened butter or nonstick cooking spray, for greasing
- 4 cups water
- 1 cup quick-cooking (not instant) grits or polenta
- 1 teaspoon seasoned salt
- 1½ cups shredded cheddar
- 4 tablespoons (½ stick) butter
- 3 eggs, well beaten
- 5 or 6 dashes Worcestershire sauce

1. Preheat the oven to 350°F. Coat a 1½-quart baking dish (I use a 7½-inch-wide round dish that's 3½ inches deep) or 6 to 8 individual ramekins or cups with softened butter.
2. Bring the water to a boil in a medium saucepan over high heat.
3. Slowly add the grits, stirring constantly. Add the seasoned salt, cooking and stirring until it returns to a boil.
4. Reduce the heat to medium-low and continue stirring until all the water is absorbed and the mixture is thick, about 5 minutes.
5. Add the cheddar and butter, stirring until melted. Slowly fold in the eggs, stirring until incorporated. Season with Worcestershire sauce and stir again.
6. Pour the mixture into the prepared dish or ramekins. Bake for 1 hour, or until nearly set but still slightly jiggly.
7. Let stand at least 10 minutes before serving.

Storage Tip

To refrigerate or freeze: Cool the soufflé, cover tightly with plastic wrap, and refrigerate for up to 4 days, or freeze for up to 3 months. (It won't be as puffy, but it will still taste great!)

To reheat: If frozen, first let it thaw in the refrigerator overnight, or until completely thawed. Remove the plastic wrap and then cover with a lid or with parchment and foil to prevent it from drying out. Place in a 350°F oven for 15 to 20 minutes, until heated through.

Norma Jean's Make-Ahead Seven-Layer Salad

SERVES 8 TO 10

If there was ever a dish that had to be made a specific way, this is it! Honestly, the back-and-forth in my family on the right way to make this salad is legendary. There are several versions floating around among my siblings, which makes it very controversial! But at Thanksgiving, this is the version that must be made. Sometimes, we have one or two more, with water chestnuts or mushrooms, which are done the "wrong way" and with the "wrong stuff," according to my mom, Norma Jean. My mom swears if you don't layer these ingredients, in this order, it won't turn out right and that it's the layering that creates the "dressing." I will never know if she's right because I'm honestly too afraid to test the theory. But you can take my word for it: This way is a winner! The beauty of this dish is that it must be made a day ahead of time and will be ready to serve straight from the fridge when festivities begin.

- 1 large head iceberg lettuce, washed, cored, and shredded
- 6 or 7 hard-boiled eggs, sliced (see Hack)
- Salt and pepper, to taste
- 1 pound bacon, crisp-cooked, drained, and crumbled (see Love Bacon, page 171)
- One 12-ounce bag frozen peas
- 1 medium red onion, sliced very thin or diced small
- ¾ cup mayonnaise
- ¾ cup Miracle Whip
- 2 to 4 tablespoons sugar, to taste
- 1 pound mild cheddar, shredded

1. The day before you plan to serve the salad, spread the lettuce in an even layer in a 9 x 13-inch glass pan or a large bowl. Layer the eggs over the lettuce and sprinkle them with salt and pepper. Sprinkle the bacon evenly on top, followed by the peas and then the onion.
2. Place the mayonnaise, Miracle Whip, and sugar in a quart-size zip-top bag and squish it around to blend the ingredients. Cut off the tip of one corner and pipe the mixture evenly over the onions. Sprinkle the cheese over the mayonnaise mixture.
3. Cover and refrigerate for 24 hours before serving to allow the flavors to meld. Do not mix before serving! Leave the layers intact and let everyone help themselves.

HACK: Making Hard-Boiled Eggs Two Ways

There are lots of theories out there on the best way to boil an egg, but here are my two faves.

Stovetop: This works best whether you've got one egg or a dozen to boil. Place the eggs in a pot and fill with water to cover by about 2 inches. Then set the burner on high. As soon as it comes to a rolling boil, cover the pan with a lid and remove it from the heat. Wait 10 minutes for a yolk that's firm but still tender (8 minutes for a softer yolk and 12 minutes for a harder one). Drain.

Oven: Yes, you read that correctly. Here's an even easier way to hard-boil a dozen eggs or more at a time: Skip the boiling by placing each egg in the cup of a muffin pan. Bake in a 325°F oven for 25 to 30 minutes.

What's the trick to peeling an egg so you don't rip it to pieces? Placing them in an ice bath will stop the cooking and make them easier to peel, especially if your eggs are very fresh. This step will make it even easier: Place the eggs, one at a time, in a mason jar or glass, cover the top with a lid or your hand, and shake until cracked all over. The shell should peel right off!

The Best Orange Fluff Ever

SERVES 6 TO 8

To folks in the Midwest and the South, anything with Jell-O in it is a salad! I don't know who started this magical tradition, but I love it and will never question it. Arlene Fearmonti, one of my mom's best friends, came up with this recipe decades ago. She literally calls it Orange Tapioca Salad, but I like the sound of "fluff," referring to its creamy, airy, yet still firm texture, even better! You can add a cup or two of mini marshmallows along with the mandarin oranges and whipped topping, if you desire. I prefer it without.

- Two 3-ounce boxes Jell-O Cook & Serve Tapioca Pudding & Pie Filling mix
- One 3-ounce box orange Jell-O Gelatin Dessert mix
- 3 cups water, divided
- One 15-ounce can mandarin oranges, drained
- One 8-ounce container nondairy whipped topping (Cool Whip or Truwhip), thawed in the refrigerator if frozen

1. Combine the pudding and gelatin mixes in a medium saucepan. Slowly stir in 1 cup water until liquified and then mix in the remaining 2 cups water.
2. Cook over medium heat, stirring constantly so it doesn't stick and scorch, until the mixture thickens slightly, 5 to 10 minutes. Remove from the stove and allow it to cool and set for 1 hour.
3. Stir in the mandarin oranges and whipped topping until everything is blended well. Cover and refrigerate, preferably overnight, or for several hours.

Lora
FIED

CHAPTER 8

Sweet Finishes

I'm a holiday gal, so I've always loved hosting and celebrating things. I'm a huge birthday person and a gift-wrapping pro to this day! In my mind, these occasions legally require something sweet and special. The other days of the year, I'm super conscientious about watching my sugar intake, but these special days are filed under "you have to live a little"! With that said, I've also found ways to take care of my sweet tooth with low-carb options for when it's just a normal Tuesday and I'm feeling like a treat. Here is a selection of my absolute faves for every occasion and sweet-tooth craving—from small bites like my low-carb Reese's Peanut Butter Cups dupe (page 234) to deceptively easy showstoppers where I get fancy with my piping bag. As you probably know by now, I see no shame in taking shortcuts: from cake and pudding mixes to dough from a tube. In the pages that follow, I show various ways to elevate them—often by pairing them with an easy, made-from-scratch frosting. Besides cakes, I'm also sharing some favorite pies, cookies, candy, and other desserts that are high in satisfaction and low in labor!

Potato Chip Cookies

MAKES ABOUT 24

The marriage of a potato chip and a cookie should probably be illegal! The cookie is tender, buttery, and nutty like a pecan sandy, with the salty crunch from the chips that's extra hard to resist. That old Lay's potato chip commercial, "Betcha can't eat just one," is doubly true in this case!

- 3½ ounces salted potato chips (regular, kettle-cooked, or ruffled)
- 1 cup (2 sticks) salted butter, softened
- ½ cup granulated sugar
- 1 tablespoon vanilla extract
- 1¾ cups all-purpose flour
- 1 cup chopped pecans
- ¼ to ½ cup powdered sugar

1. Set two racks in the middle and lower-middle levels of the oven. Preheat the oven to 350°F. Line two baking sheets with parchment paper.
2. Place the potato chips in a quart-size zip-top bag and roll over with a rolling pin until coarsely crushed. (You should have 1 cup.) Or do this in a food processor.
3. Place the butter, sugar, and vanilla in the bowl of a stand mixer fitted with a paddle attachment, or in a large bowl if using an electric hand mixer. Blend on medium speed until light and fluffy, 3 or 4 minutes.
4. Reduce the speed to low and then add the potato chips and flour. Slowly increase the speed and mix until just incorporated, taking care not to overmix. Stir in the pecans.
5. Roll the dough into balls the size of walnuts, set a few inches apart on the baking sheets, and flatten with a fork in a crisscross pattern.
6. Bake for 8 minutes. Then rotate the baking sheets front to back and top to bottom. Return to the oven and bake 8 to 10 minutes longer, until the cookies are just beginning to turn golden around the edges.
7. Allow the cookies to cool on the baking sheets for 1 minute and then dust lightly with powdered sugar.

Storage Tip

Store in an airtight container with parchment paper between layers at room temperature for up to 5 days.

The Easiest Gingerbread Cookies Ever

MAKES 18 TO 24

I remember when Pillsbury's refrigerated gingerbread dough used to save me serious life minutes during the holiday season. Nowadays, though, it's only sold in a limited edition in select markets and sells out fast. Thankfully, they offer a recipe to recreate it, using their sugar cookie dough, that's way easier than making gingerbread cookies from scratch and tastes even better. No one will believe this was born out of packaged refrigerated dough!

- One 16.5-ounce package refrigerated sugar cookie dough, room temperature
- 2 tablespoons molasses
- ⅓ cup all-purpose flour, plus more for dusting
- ¾ teaspoon ground cinnamon
- ¾ teaspoon ground ginger
- ¼ teaspoon ground allspice
- ¼ teaspoon ground cloves

1. Place the cookie dough and molasses in the bowl of a stand mixer fitted with a paddle attachment and mix until combined. Add the flour, cinnamon, ginger, allspice, and cloves and mix until completely incorporated.
2. Divide the dough in half, form into two discs, wrap each disc with plastic wrap, and refrigerate for 2 hours.
3. Preheat the oven to 375°F. Line a baking sheet with parchment paper.
4. Roll out the dough on a floured surface to ¼ inch thickness. With floured cookie cutters, cut the dough into the desired shapes. Place the cookies on the baking sheet, 2 inches apart. Bake for 7 to 9 minutes, until they are set and lightly golden brown around the edges.
5. Let cool on the baking sheet for 3 minutes. Then transfer to a wire rack to cool completely, about 20 minutes, before decorating as you wish.

Storage Tip

Store in an airtight container with parchment paper between layers at room temperature for up to 5 days. Or stack them with parchment paper between each layer and place in an airtight container or freezer-safe bag. Store in the freezer for up to 3 months.

Chocolate Chip Cookie Cups

MAKES 24 LARGE OR 48 MINI COOKIE CUPS

Who's tired of fishing for that one piece of cookie at the bottom of the glass of milk? Especially if you're like me and only have milk when it's paired with a cookie or brownie. If the cookie and milk combo isn't your thing, these cookie-cupcake babies make the perfect tiny vehicles for whipped cream, ice cream, frosting—you name it. Aside from adding an extra layer of deliciousness, coating the insides with chocolate will help guard against leakage. Feel free to adapt with any slice-and-bake type of cookie dough—just follow the time and temperature on your recipe or the package you're using. The only difference here is the shaping. If chocolate is involved, I like to add a pinch of flaky sea salt before baking to take these puppies from coach to first class!

Nonstick cooking spray

One 16.5-ounce package refrigerated chocolate chip (or other flavor) cookie dough, cut into 24 slices or rolled into balls

Flaky sea salt, optional

1 cup chocolate chips, optional

1 cup milk (any kind) or whipped cream, ice cream, or frosting, to serve

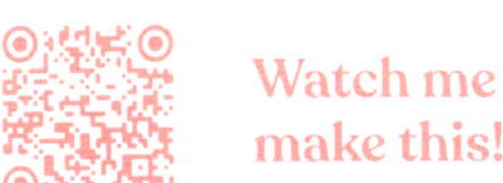
Watch me make this!

1. Preheat the oven to 350°F. Coat 24 regular or 48 mini muffin cups with cooking spray. Double them up with another pan or set them on a baking sheet to keep the cookies from burning.
2. Press raw cookie dough into the bottom of each regular-size muffin cup or cut each raw cookie in half and press each half into the bottom of a mini muffin cup with your thumb or a small spoon. Add a pinch of salt to each, if using.
3. Bake for 8 to 11 minutes, until golden brown. Immediately press an indentation into each with a wooden spoon to create a cup shape.
4. If desired, fill each indentation with 8 to 12 chocolate chips and let stand for about 2 minutes until melted. (Return to the oven for 30 seconds or so, if needed, to fully melt the chips.)
5. Spread the melted chocolate with the back of a spoon to coat the inside of each cookie cup to prevent leaks. Let cool for 15 more minutes, transfer the cookies to a tray, and refrigerate to set the chocolate.
6. Fill each cup with milk, whipped cream, ice cream, frosting, or whatever filling you choose.

Storage Tip

Store the unfilled cookie cups in an airtight container at room temperature for up to 5 days. Or stack them, standing upright, with parchment paper between each layer and place in an airtight container or freezer-safe bag. Store in the freezer for up to 3 months.

HACK: Easy Chocolatiering

I used to shy away from making chocolates because it seemed daunting. Then I discovered these tricks using an ice cube tray and a mini muffin pan, and now my family thinks I'm a chocolatier! These two recipes are for folks who never thought they could make fudge: no boiling, no candy thermometer, and heck, we're not even turning the stove on. And in both cases, you can keep these low-carb and keto by using 72 percent (or higher) sugar-free dark chocolate and zero-sugar add-ins, if desired. Macadamia nuts would be a great keto/low-carb add-in.

Chocolate Peanut Butter Cups

MAKES 12 LARGE OR 24 SMALL CANDIES

I make these low-carb by using sugar-free chocolate chips and unsweetened peanut butter, and they are beyond delicious! But truly, any kind of either will work—use what you have! I love that they even have the famous Reese's ridges on the edges.

- One 10-ounce bag regular or sugar-free chocolate chips (a little more than 1½ cups)
- ¾ cup unsweetened nut or seed butter (I use chunky peanut butter)

1. Line one regular-size or two mini muffin pans with cupcake liners.
2. Place the chocolate and nut butter in a microwave-safe bowl. Microwave on high, stirring every 30 seconds, until melted, 1½ to 2 minutes.
3. Pour into the cupcake liners and freeze for 30 minutes, or until set. Pop them out and store in an airtight container in the fridge for up to 2 weeks or in the freezer for up to 3 months. (Thaw in the fridge before eating so the paper doesn't tear.)

Ice Cube Tray Chocolates

MAKES 12

No need to get a special mold for these chocolates; an ice cube tray will do the trick—any size!

- 1 cup chocolate (any kind, chips or a bar), broken into small pieces
- ¼ cup coconut oil

ADD-INS

- Candies
- Finely chopped nuts
- Sprinkles

1. Place the chocolate and coconut oil in a microwave-safe bowl. Microwave on high in 30-second intervals, stirring each time, until melted and smooth.
2. Place ½ to 1 teaspoon of add-ins into each ice cube mold. Pour the melted chocolate on top. Freeze for at least 30 minutes.
3. Store in an airtight container in the refrigerator for up to 2 weeks, or in the freezer for up to 3 months. Thaw the chocolates in the refrigerator for at least 8 hours, then bring them to room temperature on the counter for about an hour before eating. (Chocolates made with coconut oil are subject to melting at room temperature, so don't leave them out too long.)

Blue Ribbon Frozen Margarita Pie

SERVES 6

What's the first drink that comes to mind when someone mentions Cinco de Mayo? A margarita, right? Although I don't really like the taste of alcohol, I do love the idea of chips and margs, as evidenced by this recipe. I've been making this pie for more than three decades and actually won first place in a pie contest with it! If you like margaritas, this hack is for you—without question, it's my favorite pie of all time. The best part is there's no baking and you don't even need to pull out your mixer!

CRUST

1 tablespoon softened butter

1½ cups finely crushed pretzels

½ cup plus 2 tablespoons (1¼ sticks) melted butter

¼ cup sugar

FILLING

One 14-ounce can sweetened condensed milk

⅓ cup lime juice

¼ cup tequila

2 tablespoons Triple Sec or Cointreau

One 8-ounce container Cool Whip or ½ pint heavy whipping cream, whipped to medium peaks

1 drop each of yellow and green food coloring, optional

TOPPING

1 lime, sliced, optional

1. **MAKE THE CRUST:** Rub the softened butter inside a 9-inch glass pie plate. Mix the pretzel crumbs, melted butter, and sugar in a medium bowl and then press the mixture into the pie plate to coat the bottom and sides.
2. **MAKE THE FILLING:** Mix the sweetened condensed milk, lime juice, tequila, and Triple Sec in a large bowl. Then fold in the whipped cream and food coloring, if using.
3. Pour the filling into the crust, cover with plastic or foil, and freeze for at least 4 hours before serving. Wrapped well, the pie may be frozen for up to 4 months.
4. Top with lime slices if desired, and serve.

Fast and Fancy Cinnamon-Caramel Apple Pie

SERVES 6 TO 8

Are you more of a pie person or a cinnamon roll fan? Why choose?! Now you don't have to. And don't feel limited to apple. This crust would be insane on a pecan pie!

- Softened butter or nonstick cooking spray, for greasing
- All-purpose flour, for dusting
- One 12.4-ounce can refrigerated Pillsbury Cinnamon Rolls (8 count)
- Two 21-ounce cans apple pie filling
- 2 or 3 tablespoons caramel sauce or topping (from a bottle or a jar), to taste
- One 14.1-ounce package refrigerated pie crust (2 crusts)
- 1 large egg, beaten
- 1 tablespoon heavy cream or water
- 1 to 2 teaspoons sugar
- Flaky sea salt, to taste

1. Preheat the oven to 375°F. Butter a 9-inch pie plate and set aside. Sprinkle a surface with flour.
2. Pop open the can of cinnamon rolls and set the tub of icing aside. Cut each roll in half across the center and dust on both sides with the flour. Set each piece on the floured surface and roll to about ⅛ inch thickness, taking care not to tear the dough.
3. Lay each piece in the bottom and up the sides of the pie plate, pressing the edges together. Press into the pie plate.
4. Pour the apple pie filling into the pie plate. Top the filling with the caramel sauce (measure with your heart here).
5. Unroll one of the pie dough sheets onto the floured surface. If desired, use a small cookie cutter of your choice to cut a few shapes out of the center of the dough, and set the cutouts aside. Lay the dough sheet with the holes over the filling, making sure to pinch the edges together. Then arrange the cut pieces decoratively on top of the crust, leaving the holes exposed.
6. Make an egg wash by combining the egg and cream in a small bowl.
7. Unroll the second pie dough sheet and cut out additional pieces with your cookie cutter for the edge of your crust. Brush the edge of the dough in the pan with egg wash and then place the cutouts on top to form a thick crust.
8. Brush the entire top of the pie with a little egg wash and sprinkle with sugar and a little bit of sea salt.
9. Cover the edges with a pie protector or foil, place on a baking sheet, and bake for 40 to 50 minutes, until golden brown and bubbly.
10. Cool completely before cutting. If you like, drizzle some of the reserved icing over each slice.

Storage Tip

You can keep this pie on the counter, covered, for up to 2 days. Or wrap in plastic wrap and store in the refrigerator for up to 3 days. You can also wrap it in plastic wrap and then foil and freeze for up to 3 months. Thaw overnight in the refrigerator or on the counter for an hour or so before reheating. Reheat in a 350°F oven for 15 to 20 minutes, loosely covered with parchment and foil to prevent overbrowning, until bubbly.

SABRE

Fruit Crisp on the Grill

SERVES 4 TO 6

For your next cookout, here's a fabulous dessert you can cook up while everyone's eating and the grill is still hot! In the dead of summer, feel free to swap out the apples for peaches, berries, or whatever fruit you like. And don't forget the ice cream!

FILLING

2 large Honeycrisp or green apples, peeled and sliced, or 3 to 4 peeled and sliced peaches

¼ cup packed brown sugar

2 tablespoons granulated sugar (or less, depending on your sweet tooth and the sweetness of your fruit)

1 tablespoon cold butter, cut into small pieces

2 teaspoons cornstarch

2 teaspoons lemon juice

1 teaspoon ground cinnamon

1 teaspoon vanilla extract

TOPPING

¼ cup packed brown sugar

¼ cup all-purpose flour

¼ cup rolled oats

½ teaspoon ground cinnamon

Pinch of salt

¼ cup (½ stick) cold butter

Vanilla ice cream, for serving

1. Preheat the grill to 350°F.
2. **MAKE THE FILLING:** Stir together the fruit, brown sugar, granulated sugar, butter, cornstarch, lemon juice, cinnamon, and vanilla in a large bowl until the fruit is coated.
3. **MAKE THE TOPPING**: Stir together the brown sugar, flour, oats, cinnamon, and salt in a medium bowl. Grate the butter with a box grater into the bowl and stir to combine. (It will be lumpy and crumbly.)
4. Tear off four sheets of foil and four sheets of parchment, each about 10 × 12 inches. Lay two sheets of foil (dull side up) onto a work surface and line each with a sheet of parchment.
5. Divide the fruit mixture between them and crumble the topping over each. Lay another sheet of parchment and then foil (dull side down) on top of each bundle, tucking the corners in and up to seal. (The parchment will keep the crisp from taking on a "tinny" taste as it cooks.)
6. Cook on the grill for 12 to 15 minutes. Let the packets cool for about 10 minutes before opening. Serve with ice cream.

Pumpkin Spice Delight Cake

SERVES 10 TO 12

This is my favorite fall dessert, and it's so easy! It's the ugly cake everyone loves. I first came across it in some old community cookbook, where it was called Pumpkin Dump Cake, and decided to serve it for a luncheon I cohosted for a large group of ladies. But since Pumpkin Dump Cake didn't sound "elevated" enough, I changed the name to Pumpkin Spice Delight, and it was a huge hit. I got so many requests for the recipe that I had to create a note in my phone so I could text and email people on the spot. I made it for a Halloween party and changed the name again—this time to Pumpkin Spooky Cake. When I posted it on Instagram, I promised that while it looks like a trick, it's an amazing treat. Countless followers made it and told me they agreed! I've even made it in individual ramekins for parties. If you really want to get crazy, scoop some ice cream on top.

Softened butter or nonstick cooking spray, for greasing

One 15-ounce can pumpkin puree

One 12-ounce can evaporated milk

1 cup packed brown sugar

3 large eggs

2 teaspoons pumpkin pie spice

One 15.25-ounce box yellow cake mix

1 cup chopped pecans

1 cup (2 sticks) salted butter, melted

1. Preheat the oven to 350°F. Butter the bottom and sides of a 9 x 13-inch baking pan.
2. Combine the pumpkin puree, evaporated milk, brown sugar, eggs, and pumpkin pie spice in a large bowl. Whisk until combined. Pour the mixture into the prepared pan.
3. Sprinkle the cake mix on top of the batter and then sprinkle the pecans over the batter. Pour the melted butter evenly over the top of the cake.
4. Bake for 45 to 50 minutes, until the edges are browned, the center is set, and a knife inserted in the middle comes out clean.

A Note About Cake Mix Sizes

Most standard cake mixes today, such as Duncan Hines, have shrunk from 18.25 ounces to 15.25 ounces. Some brands, including Betty Crocker, have shrunk even further, to 13.25 ounces. Most of these recipes were tested with Duncan Hines except for a couple where I thought the Better Crocker brand worked best. While fairly interchangeable, the outcomes—and yields—will be slightly different so it's best to go with the box size specified.

Storage Tip

Wrap the cooled cake in its pan in plastic wrap, or cut in pieces and place in airtight containers. Store at room temperature for up to 3 days, in the refrigerator for up to 5 days, or in the freezer with plastic wrap and a layer of foil for up to 3 months. Thaw in the refrigerator overnight before serving. Serve it chilled, room temperature, or warmed in the oven for 5 to 10 minutes.

Coca-Cola
CONT. NET. 355 ml
355ml

Coca-Cola Cake
with Pourable Fudge Frosting

SERVES 8 TO 12

Many years ago, my mother sent me her recipe for a 100 percent made-from-scratch Chocolate Coke Cake in the form of a typewritten letter that began with "Dearest Lora" and ended with "Good luck! Love, Mom." I still have it among my keepsakes. The fact that the recipe ended with "good luck" tells you everything you need to know. There had to be a hack for this one! Luckily, there is: This recipe has all the ooey-gooey goodness of the dreamy cola cake, like the one from Cracker Barrel, without all the luck needed from Mom.

CAKE

Nonstick cooking spray

One 15.25-ounce box chocolate cake mix

One 12-ounce can Coca-Cola

GLAZE

1 cup chocolate chips

⅓ cup mini marshmallows

4 tablespoons (½ stick) salted butter

1. Preheat the oven to 350°F. Spray a 9 x 13-inch pan with cooking spray.
2. **MAKE THE CAKE:** Pour the cake mix and cola into a large bowl and mix with an electric hand mixer or a whisk until smooth.
3. Pour the batter into the prepared baking pan. Bake for 35 to 40 minutes, until a toothpick inserted in the center comes out clean.
4. **MEANWHILE, MAKE THE GLAZE:** Place the chocolate chips, marshmallows, and butter in a small saucepan over low heat, stirring until melted and smooth, 3 or 4 minutes. (Or place the ingredients in a microwave-safe bowl and heat, checking and stirring every 30 seconds, until melted.)
5. Pour over the warm cake and let cool.

Storage Tip

Wrap the cooled cake in its pan in plastic wrap, or cut in pieces and place in airtight containers. Store at room temperature for up to 3 days, in the refrigerator for up to 5 days, or in the freezer with plastic wrap and a layer of foil for up to 3 months. Thaw in the refrigerator overnight before serving.

Malibu Sunshine Cake

SERVES 10 TO 12

If Malibu Barbie had a non-pink cake, I'm convinced this would be it! It's truly like a slice of sunshine. And here's the kicker: I'm not really a pineapple or angel food cake gal, but I love this cake! It has a soufflé-like texture and tastes like vacation. With only two ingredients and almost zero effort, you'll look like a baking superstar! Don't think of this as a conventional angel food cake. I bake mine in a glass Pyrex dish (don't use metal—it's more likely to stick). It's great for potlucks or for snacking straight out of the fridge. Top with whipped cream or serve as is.

- One 20-ounce can crushed pineapple with juice
- One 16-ounce box angel food cake mix ("add water only" version)
- Whipped cream, optional
- Sprinkles, for garnish, optional

1. Preheat the oven to 350°F. Stir together the pineapple (with the juice) and cake mix until smooth and creamy and pour into a 9 x 13-inch glass baking pan.
2. Bake for 25 minutes, or until a toothpick inserted in the center comes out clean. It will come out puffy and settle as it cools. Serve with whipped cream and garnish with sprinkles, if desired.

Storage Tip

Wrap the cooled cake in its pan in plastic wrap or cut in pieces and place in airtight containers. Store in the refrigerator for up to 3 days. This cake is delicious served warm, at room temperature, or straight out of the fridge. (It can be frozen, but because it contains no fat, it dries out quickly and I don't recommend it.)

Coffee House Iced Lemon Loaf

MAKES ONE 9 X 5-INCH LOAF

If you had ten bucks in your wallet, would you rather have two slices of iced lemon loaf or two pans of it? Trick question, I know! Here's the most amazing copycat Starbucks lemon loaf recipe out there! It's easy and affordable. It's also beautiful. You can take this to a potluck or make it in advance and freeze for later. I like slicing it up and freezing for a grab-and-go treat. The best part is that it doesn't have any of the crazy ingredients you don't recognize in the one from "you-know-who." (Thanks to Kristyn Merkley of @lillunakristyn for the inspo for this one.)

CAKE

Nonstick cooking spray

One 3.4-ounce box Jell-O Lemon Instant Pudding & Pie Filling mix

1½ cups all-purpose flour

½ teaspoon baking powder

½ teaspoon baking soda

½ teaspoon salt

1 cup granulated sugar

1 tablespoon grated lemon zest

¾ cup sour cream or plain yogurt

½ cup avocado oil or other neutral oil

⅓ cup lemon juice

3 large eggs

2 tablespoons softened butter

1 teaspoon vanilla extract

ICING

1½ cups powdered sugar

3 tablespoons softened butter

3 tablespoons lemon juice

1. **MAKE THE CAKE:** Preheat the oven to 350°F. Coat a 9 x 5-inch loaf pan with cooking spray.
2. Whisk the pudding mix, flour, baking powder, baking soda, and salt in a medium bowl.
3. Mix the granulated sugar and lemon zest in a large bowl. Add the sour cream, oil, lemon juice, eggs, butter, and vanilla. Blend with an electric hand mixer at medium speed just until blended.
4. Slowly add the dry mixture to the wet mixture and blend just until smooth.
5. Pour the batter into the loaf pan, leaving a 1¼-inch space between the batter and the top. Bake for 55 minutes, or until a toothpick inserted in the middle comes out clean.
6. Let cool in the pan for 10 minutes and then remove from the pan and let cool completely on a wire rack.
7. **MAKE THE ICING:** Place the powdered sugar, butter, and lemon juice in a medium bowl and mix with an electric hand mixer on low to medium speed until blended and smooth. Pour the icing over the cooled loaf.

Storage Tip

Store the cooled cake in an airtight container or wrapped in plastic wrap for up to 3 days at room temperature or up to a week in the refrigerator. Or freeze the cake (without icing) wrapped in plastic wrap and a layer of foil for up to 3 months. Allow the cake to thaw overnight in the refrigerator, bring to room temperature, and then add the icing before serving.

One-Pan, Three-Layer, Triple-Chocolate Cake

SERVES 8 TO 18 (DEPENDING ON HOW YOU SLICE IT)

Have you ever tried to bake three even layers of cake, without that hump that forms in the middle? Or maybe one of the layers came out either too thick or too thin? This recipe uses a super-simple baking hack that solves either of those problems! To make it, you'll need an 18 x 13 x 1-inch baking sheet and an 8-inch cake ring. Once you try it, you'll never be intimidated to make a multilayer, bakery-worthy feat again!

- 4 large eggs
- 1 cup avocado oil or other neutral oil
- 1 cup Greek yogurt
- ½ cup milk (any kind)
- 1 teaspoon vanilla extract
- One 15.25-ounce box devil's food cake mix
- One 3.4-ounce box Jell-O Cook & Serve Instant Chocolate Pudding & Pie Filling mix
- 2 teaspoons ground cinnamon
- One 12-ounce bag chocolate chips
- 2 batches Chocolate Buttercream Frosting (see page 260)

Watch me make this!

1. Preheat the oven to 350°F. Line a rimmed 13 x 18-inch baking sheet with parchment cut so it goes up the lip by an inch to prevent leaking.
2. Crack the eggs into a large bowl. Beat on medium speed with an electric hand mixer until well blended and then beat in the oil, yogurt, milk, and vanilla until well combined.
3. Add the cake mix, pudding mix, and cinnamon, and beat until just blended. (The batter will be thick.) Fold in the chocolate chips.
4. Spread the batter in the prepared baking sheet. Bake for 25 to 35 minutes, until a toothpick comes out clean. Let cool completely. Lift the cake out of the baking sheet onto a work surface.
5. **PREPARE THE CAKE LAYERS:** Using your cake ring, cut out two full circles diagonally across the cake. Then use the rest of the space to make half circles using half of the ring (see QR code).
6. **FROST THE CAKE:** Set one whole cake layer on a cake stand or serving plate. Spoon ½ to 1 cup frosting onto the bottom layer and spread evenly to the sides with an offset spatula.
7. Place the two cake halves on top to form the second layer; add another ½ cup or so of frosting and spread to the sides. (The top layer will hide any sign of the crack where the two halves meet.)
8. Top with the other whole cake layer and then frost the top and sides of the cake with a thin layer of frosting. (If time permits, set it in the fridge for about 15 minutes to harden.) Spread with a thicker layer of frosting.
9. If you really want to get fancy, place the remaining frosting into a pastry bag fitted with a star tip and pipe chocolate roses over the entire cake.

Storage Tip

Store the frosted cake, covered, for up to 3 days on the counter, or for up to 5 days in an airtight container in the refrigerator. Once cut, use plastic wrap to cover the cut edges to prevent drying. Whole or sliced, the cake may be frozen for up to 2 months. To freeze, set the frosted cake, unwrapped, in the freezer for about 4 hours, or long enough for the frosting to set. Then wrap tightly with a layer of plastic wrap, followed by foil. (Stick individually wrapped slices in a freezer-safe bag or airtight container.)

Holiday Bundt Cake

SERVES 12 TO 14

If you were Santa, how happy would you be to be greeted by a piece of cake in lieu of yet another cookie? Though I'm a huge fan of frosted sugar cookies, especially the soft ones eaten cold, straight out of the freezer, this cake is a stunner! Plus, this beauty is affordable—it only looks expensive. And you can make this any color for any celebration. I'm thinking hot pink and green would be gorgeous for Easter! Red, white, and blue for the Fourth of July; orange, green, and a touch of purple for Halloween . . . the combinations are endless.

- Avocado oil or avocado oil spray, for greasing
- All-purpose flour, for dusting
- One 15.25-ounce box white cake mix
- 3 heaping tablespoons instant vanilla pudding mix (half of a 3.4-ounce box)
- 1 cup sour cream
- ½ cup avocado oil or other neutral oil
- ½ cup water
- 4 large egg whites
- 1½ teaspoons red food coloring, plus a few drops for frosting
- 1 teaspoon green food coloring, plus a few drops for frosting
- 1 batch Vanilla Buttercream Frosting (page 260) or one 16-ounce container vanilla frosting

1. Lightly grease and flour a 12-cup Bundt pan and set it on a baking sheet (this helps keep the bottom from burning). Set one large and two medium bowls on the counter.
2. Pour the cake mix, pudding mix, sour cream, oil, water, and egg whites into the large bowl and beat on medium speed with an electric hand mixer until well combined.
3. Leave half the batter in the large bowl and pour one-fourth of the batter into each of the two medium bowls. Whisk the red food coloring into one of the medium bowls of batter and the green coloring into the other, leaving the larger bowl of batter white.
4. Pour half of the white batter into the Bundt pan. Pour all the red batter on top, gently spreading if necessary to create an even layer but taking care not to mix the layers. Add all the green batter, followed by the remaining white batter, keeping the colors of the layers separate.
5. Slide the baking sheet (with the Bundt pan) into the cold oven and then turn on the heat to 350°F. Bake for 55 to 60 minutes, until a cake tester inserted in the center comes out clean. Remove the cake from the oven and let cool in the pan for 10 to 15 minutes.
6. Set a wire rack on a baking sheet lined with parchment paper (to catch crumbs). Transfer the cake, still in the pan, to the rack to cool, about 15 minutes. Then run a knife around the edge of the pan and carefully invert it onto the rack to cool completely, about 45 minutes. Set the cooled cake on a cake plate or cake stand.
7. **WHILE THE CAKE COOLS, PREPARE THE FROSTING:** Divide the frosting equally among three small bowls. Stir a few drops of red food coloring into the first bowl of frosting until you reach your desired shade. Repeat with the green food coloring and the second bowl of frosting. Leave the last bowl white.
8. Spoon the frostings into three sandwich bags and snip off one corner of each. Squeeze the frostings decoratively over the cake. To store for later, see Storage Tip on page 249.

Pretty in Pink Barbie Dream Cake

SERVES 12 TO 24

I remember seeing these cakes in the grocery store bakery as a child and begging for one until I finally got my wish on my ninth birthday! My Barbie cake was so special that I can remember every detail: the red-and-white frosting dress, the brunette Barbie—it was everything! I think I was the first kid to bring a cake instead of cupcakes for a class party, too! Flash forward four decades to the Barbie movie. I knew that was my sign to recreate my own dream doll cake at home. I chose a pink motif with strawberry flavor inside and out, but you're the fashion designer here and you can use any cake batter you'd like. She's so pretty, I have to admit it was a little hard to cut into her. (For a crowd, use two cake mixes and a 5-quart bowl and increase the cooking time to about 1 hour and 20 minutes.)

- Nonstick cooking spray or avocado oil, for greasing
- All-purpose flour, for dusting
- One 13.25-ounce box Betty Crocker Delights Super Moist Strawberry cake mix
- 1 cup water
- ½ cup avocado oil
- 3 large eggs
- 1 Barbie doll
- 1 batch Strawberry Buttercream or Vanilla Buttercream Frosting (page 260) or one 16-ounce container vanilla frosting mixed with 1 or 2 drops red food coloring
- Wilton sugar pearls

Watch me make this!

1. Set a rack in the lower third of the oven and remove the top rack. Preheat the oven to 325°F. Grease a 2-quart metal oven-safe mixing bowl about 10 inches in diameter (or a dome-shaped cake pan) with cooking spray; dust with flour and tap out the excess.
2. Combine the cake mix, water, oil, and eggs in a large bowl and mix with an electric hand mixer on medium speed (or beat vigorously by hand) for 2 minutes, or until thoroughly blended. Pour the batter into the prepared bowl or pan for baking.
3. Bake for 50 to 60 minutes, until a cake tester inserted in the center comes out clean. (If the cake appears to be overbrowning, reduce the temperature to 300°F.) Let the cake cool completely before removing from the pan onto a cake stand.
4. Remove Barbie's legs and insert her body into the middle of the cake. (Don't worry, you can wash her up afterward and snap those legs right back on.)
5. Scoop the frosting into a piping bag fitted with a star tip. Starting at the top of the cake, squeeze in a circular motion to form rows of rosettes, working down to the bottom. With tweezers, set a sugar pearl in the center of each rosette. To store for later, see Storage Tip on page 251.

Red Velvet Cupcakes
with Half-Homemade Cream Cheese Icing

MAKES 24

When I was little, red velvet cake was a novelty and rarely seen . . . red velvet cupcakes weren't even a thing! My mom had a recipe that used beet juice for the coloring, and honestly, it was so much work that it just wasn't in heavy rotation. The scarcity of it caused even more of a longing. Now, it is so readily available in stores, which tickles me pink (I mean red)! Even better news: Both Betty Crocker and Duncan Hines have red velvet cake mixes that are hard to improve upon, especially when you sub in buttermilk for the water to give it a little tang, heft, and extra-tender crumb. As for the topping, a not-too-sweet cream cheese frosting is a must! I have a shortcut hack for that, too: Blend extra cream cheese into store-bought cream cheese frosting for a richer, less sweet taste and a smoother texture that's just like homemade. This means you'll have more frosting than you'll need for these cupcakes, but the extra will be good in the fridge for a couple of weeks, ready to spread on toast or graham crackers or, thinned with a little milk, as a dip for fruit.

CUPCAKES

One 15.25-ounce box Duncan Hines Signature Perfectly Moist Red Velvet cake mix

1 cup low-fat buttermilk (see Note)

½ cup avocado oil or other neutral oil

3 large eggs

White nonpareils, for garnish, optional

CREAM CHEESE FROSTING

One 16-ounce container cream cheese frosting

One 8-ounce package cream cheese, softened

1. Preheat the oven to 350°F. See Hack: Avoiding Burnt Cupcake Bottoms (page 261) for optional precautions before baking. Line two 12-cup muffin pans with cupcake liners.
2. **MAKE THE CUPCAKES:** Place the cake mix, buttermilk, oil, and eggs in a large bowl and beat with an electric hand mixer at low speed until moistened, about 30 seconds, and then at medium speed for 2 minutes. Pour the batter into the muffin pans.
3. Bake for 16 to 18 minutes, until a toothpick inserted in the center comes out clean. Remove the cupcakes from the pans and let cool completely on a wire rack.
4. **MAKE THE FROSTING:** Whip the frosting with the softened cream cheese in a large bowl with an electric hand mixer on medium speed, as you would homemade frosting, until fluffy.
5. **FROST, DECORATE, AND SERVE:** Pipe or spread the frosting on the cooled cupcakes and decorate with white nonpareils or as desired.

Storage Tips

1. Once cooled, place the unfrosted cupcakes in an airtight container, with parchment paper between layers if stacking. Store at room temperature for up to 2 days. To freeze, wrap the cupcakes individually in plastic wrap, then foil, then place in an airtight container and freeze for up to 3 months. To thaw, unwrap them and bring to room temperature on the counter for a few hours. Frost and decorate as desired.
2. Refrigerate cream cheese–frosted cupcakes in an airtight container for up to 5 days. (Cream cheese frosting should be refrigerated after 2 hours to prevent spoilage.) Or set the cupcakes, uncovered, on a baking sheet in the freezer until the frosting is firm, up to 4 hours. Then individually wrap each in plastic wrap or place in an airtight container and freeze for up to 3 months. Let them thaw overnight in the refrigerator, then set on the counter for about an hour before serving to soften a bit.

Confetti Cake and Ice Cream Cupcakes

MAKES 14

Are you team cake or team ice cream? With this super easy hack, you no longer need to choose! These are quick and delicious and are the moistest cupcakes I've ever had! Any cake mix and ice cream flavor will work, so long as they are similar or complementary in flavor and the ice cream is full-fat. It's just the thing for a birthday party. For this recipe, I used the smaller Betty Crocker mix to work with a one-pint container of ice cream. If you use a 15.25-ounce box, you'll need to add another half-cup or so of melted ice cream to reach a cake batter consistency. That would make about 20 cupcakes.

- One 13.25-ounce box confetti cake mix (or any flavor)
- One pint full-fat confetti cake ice cream or vanilla ice cream (or any flavor), melted (2 cups)
- Chocolate, Vanilla, or Strawberry Buttercream Frosting (page 260) or Cream Cheese Frosting (see page 256)
- Sprinkles and birthday candles, optional

1. Preheat the oven to 350°F. See Hack: Avoiding Burnt Cupcake Bottoms (page 261) for optional precautions before baking. Line a 12-cup muffin pan, plus two cups in a second pan, with cupcake liners.
2. Place the cake mix and ice cream in a bowl and whisk until smooth (see Headnote if you're using a larger box of cake mix).
3. Pour the batter into the prepared muffin pans and bake for 16 to 18 minutes, until a toothpick inserted in the center comes out clean. Remove the cupcakes from the pans and let cool completely on a wire rack.
4. Once cooled, frost with the frosting and decorate as desired.

Storage Tip

Place buttercream-frosted cupcakes in an airtight container and store at room temperature for up to 3 days or refrigerate for up to 5 days. (But the fridge tends to dry them out quicker, so stick to the counter for as long as you can.) Follow freezing and thawing instructions as for cream cheese-frosted cupcakes (see page 256).

HACK: DIY Cupcake Carrier

Need to transport your cupcakes but worry about them sliding around? Here's an easy solution, and all it takes is a baking sheet and some Scotch tape or painter's tape. Simply stretch pieces of tape from one side of the pan to the other lengthwise and crosswise so each cupcake has its own box to hold it in place! See photo on page 226.

Vanilla Buttercream Frosting

MAKES ENOUGH FROSTING FOR 12 TO 18 CUPCAKES OR ONE 9 X 13-INCH SHEET CAKE (SEE TIP)

Are you a frosting person or cake person? A good clue: If you ask for a corner, you're a frosting fan, and if you head for the middle piece, you're more of a cake aficionado. Then there's me . . . I'm a frosting snob. Yep, I'll admit it, if the frosting isn't good, I'll take my fork and scrape it off to get to the cake. The reverse is also true: If the frosting is good, the cake just becomes the vehicle for the frosting. While I'm not above using store-bought frosting, especially when time is limited (organic cream cheese is my go-to), I love a simple homemade frosting. Here are my tried-and-true buttercream frostings for when you've got a little more time. My trick for vanilla buttercream: Add just enough lemon juice to tame the sweetness and brighten the flavor without overpowering the vanilla.

- 1 cup (2 sticks) salted butter, softened
- ¼ teaspoon salt
- 4 cups powdered sugar, measured and then sifted, divided
- 3 tablespoons heavy cream or whole milk
- 2 to 3 teaspoons pure vanilla extract
- 1 teaspoon fresh lemon juice

1. Place the butter and salt in a large bowl and beat on medium speed with an electric hand mixer or a stand mixer fitted with a paddle attachment for 2 minutes.
2. Add 2 cups sugar and continue beating until well combined, about 2 more minutes. Add the remaining 2 cups sugar and beat again until fully combined, about 2 more minutes.
3. Add the cream, vanilla, and lemon juice and whip until smooth and fluffy.

Tip

Make 1½ times the recipe for a two-layer cake. Double the recipe for a triple-layer cake or for extra frosting for piping on a double-layer cake.

Storage Tip

Store in an airtight container in the refrigerator for up to a week, or in the freezer for up to 3 months. Thaw in the refrigerator overnight or at room temperature for 30 to 45 minutes before using and then rewhip to bring it back to life.

Chocolate Buttercream Frosting

Omit the lemon juice, cut the powdered sugar to 3 cups, and add ½ cup cocoa powder.

Strawberry or Raspberry Buttercream Frosting

Grind 1 cup freeze-dried strawberries or raspberries in a food processor into powdery crumbs (about ½ cup). Sift out the seeds—don't worry if you can't catch them all! Fold in the powdered berries in step 2.

Champagne Buttercream Frosting

Increase the powdered sugar to 4½ cups, reduce the heavy cream to 2 tablespoons, and replace the vanilla with ¼ cup champagne, prosecco, or any sparkling wine. (Add ½ teaspoon grated lemon zest, if desired).

Champagne Cupcakes

MAKES 18 TO 24

Would you rather eat this sparkly treat or drink it? I'm definitely in the "eat it" category! Don't worry: The bubbly bakes out so anyone can eat these cupcakes. But if you'd like to skip the champagne altogether, you can use ginger ale, sparkling apple cider, or sparkling grape juice—just note that the taste will be a bit sweeter. I use prosecco in this recipe because it's the most budget friendly.

- One 15.25-ounce box white cake mix
- 1 cup champagne, prosecco, or sparkling wine (or ginger ale)
- ½ cup avocado oil or other neutral oil
- 3 large eggs
- Champagne Buttercream Frosting (see page 260)
- Silver or gold sprinkles and sparkler candles, optional

1. Preheat the oven to 350°F. See Hack: Avoiding Burnt Cupcake Bottoms for optional precautions before baking. Line two 12-cup muffin pans with cupcake liners.
2. **MAKE THE CUPCAKES:** Place the cake mix, champagne, oil, and eggs in a large bowl and beat with an electric hand mixer at low speed until moistened, about 30 seconds, and then at medium speed for 2 minutes. Pour the batter into the muffin pans.
3. Bake for 16 to 18 minutes, until a toothpick inserted in the center comes out clean. Remove the cupcakes from the pans and let cool completely on a wire rack.
4. Frost with the Champagne Buttercream Frosting and decorate as desired.
5. To store for later, see Storage Tips on pages 256 and 257.

HACK: Avoiding Burnt Cupcake Bottoms

Do you sometimes end up with cupcakes with burnt bottoms even when you follow the recipe to a T? It can help to use lighter-colored pans, which absorb less heat than darker ones, and bake in the center of the oven or adjust your oven rack so it's not too close to the bottom heating element. But you can do more.

Here are two hacks I strongly recommend. Try one or both!

Double-pan your muffins—that is, stack your lined pan on top of an empty pan for an extra layer of insulation and more even heat distribution. Placing your muffin pan on top of a baking sheet should also do the trick.

Sprinkle a teaspoon or so of dried rice into the bottom of each cup before adding the liners. The rice absorbs some of the heat to help prevent burning and any excess moisture and fat that would sink down and make the liners greasy.

Simplified Baked Alaska

SERVES 6 TO 8

Baked Alaska is one of the most difficult-sounding desserts on the planet! So when Mrs. Rhode announced we'd be making one in our sixth-grade home ec class, a collective audible sigh echoed through the room. How on earth could tweens pull this off? Up until now, our biggest challenge had been trying to floss between the braces on our teeth. But Mrs. Rhode was a smart cookie (pun intended). She knew this was an easy one that would surely get our attention, and she was right! The pride we felt pulling that gently browned dome of still-frozen ice cream out of a piping hot oven made us feel like Houdini! I'll never forget that feeling, and I want you to have it, too. It's way easier than you think: Start with a single-layer cake or piece together slices of pound cake to form a round cake. Then let the freezer do the work while you whip up a meringue. Cover your frozen dome, and set it in the oven for a few minutes, just long enough to toast the peaks. Then prepare for the round of applause sure to greet you at the table!

Nonstick cooking spray

1 pint chocolate ice cream (or flavor of choice)

1 pint pistachio ice cream (or flavor of choice)

1 pint strawberry ice cream (or flavor of choice)

One 8- or 9-inch round prepared yellow or chocolate cake (or pound cake slices), frozen, to make a stable base

MERINGUE

6 large egg whites, room temperature

¼ teaspoon cream of tartar

1 cup sugar

½ teaspoon vanilla extract

1. Clear out ample space in your freezer to accommodate a 3-quart bowl, 8 or 9 inches in diameter (to match the size of your cake base).
2. Coat the inside of the bowl with cooking spray and line with plastic wrap, leaving about 6 inches of overhang around the edges. Let the ice cream soften slightly, then quickly pack scoops, alternating the flavors, into the bowl. Flatten with an offset spatula and fold the plastic wrap overhang over the top. Place in the freezer until completely firm, at least 4 hours.
3. If using the oven, set a rack on the bottom, allowing about 12 inches of headspace from the broiler. Preheat the broiler to high. Line a large ovenproof plate, baking sheet, or other large pan (I use a round pizza pan) with parchment paper or foil and set the frozen cake on top.
4. **MAKE THE MERINGUE:** Place the egg whites in the bowl of a stand mixer fitted with a whisk attachment (or use a handheld mixer and a large bowl). Add the cream of tartar and whip on medium-high speed until foamy, 1 or 2 minutes.
5. Increase the speed to high and beat in the sugar, 1 tablespoon at a time, until the meringue is glossy and forms stiff peaks. Fold in the vanilla.
6. Remove the bowl from the freezer. Peel back the plastic wrap and gently invert the bowl onto the cake. Remove the bowl and the plastic wrap. Working quickly, heap the meringue onto the ice cream and gently spread it with an offset spatula to cover completely, swirling decoratively to form peaks.
7. Set the pan with the cake in the oven, if using, for 3 to 4 minutes, just until the meringue tips are lightly browned. Or toast the meringue with a kitchen torch. Serve immediately, using a knife dipped in hot water to cut the slices.

Storage Tip

If you've got the freezer space, you can place the entire assembled Alaska (before toasting or torching the meringue) in the freezer, uncovered, for at least 2 hours, or up to 2 days, to set the meringue. Brown the meringue just before serving. Leftover Baked Alaska will keep in the freezer, wrapped in plastic and foil and/or in an airtight container, for about a month.

Index

D

E

F

G

H

I

J

K

L

M

N

T

U

Y

Z

Acknowledgments

Along with my parents and the family I'm feeding and raising today (to whom this book is dedicated), there are so many other people I am grateful to for helping me make this book—and my life—possible.

My siblings (listed alphabetically—no favoritism here!): **Cherri, Debi, Denny, Kay, Sandi, Susie, Tim,** and **Tre**. From the time I became your unexpected baby sister, I learned the power of home-cooked meals prepared with love and shared around the family dining room table.

Anica Petrovic, who I call Kid 1.5. Thank you for being a part of our crazy family, sis, and for helping to convince me the "adulting" tips I gave you and Betsy (Kid 1) in college deserved a larger audience. You know how much you mean to all of us; we love you!

Dr. Apostolos Lekkos. I'll never forget what you told me during my yearly exam in 2020: "In the next six months I prescribe for you to go figure something out, live your passion, and just 'be you.'" A few months later, LORAfied was born.

Cathy Doyle and **Jamie Raab.** It was you who took my hand and started me walking down this path, asking for nothing in return. Just two incredible women in the world of publishing helping a cookbook newbie get her start.

Karen Murgolo, my literary agent, who understood me from the start and was on board with the LORAfied mission. In a world of sixteen-ingredient recipes, thank you for taking a chance on the gal who thinks salt and pepper are sexy.

Susan Puckett. You kept me on track and gently reminded me "measure with your heart" needs to be a little more specific when it comes to a cookbook recipe. I couldn't have done this without you, sister! I'm pretty sure if we started comparing family trees, we'd be related.

Chynna Williams, my right-hand gal, who always has my back. No one would believe the crazy situations we put ourselves in to get "the shot" for my videos! I don't know what I'd do without you, sis!

Anthony Zuiker. Your encouragement from the beginning to just keep going, even when others had yet to see the vision, was everything! I will be forever grateful.

Mike Schibel. Even in my TV days, you knew I should be doing something different. Thank you for encouraging me down this road.

Olivia Peluso, my amazing editor, you are a gift! Thank you for all of your support and spunk! Your vision, your guidance, your passion—I'm beyond grateful for all of it.

Ivan Solis. I couldn't have asked for a better photographer to capture my vision. Your attention to even the smallest detail, like choosing which Barbie doll spoke to the camera the best, is mind-blowing! Thank you, **Matthew Brockman** and **Justin Bordeaux,** for making my recipes jump off the page!

Marian Cairns. To say you channeled me while cooking and styling my recipes for photography would be an understatement, sister! From the moment I saw you make my Blue Ribbon Frozen Margarita Pie, I knew we were a culinary mind meld. Thank you, **Jen Bolbat** and **Paige Arnett,** for absolutely nailing every single recipe for the camera!

Amy Paliwoda. Your knack for creating a moment and setting a scene left me in awe! From the placement of a teacup to the turn of a vase of flowers, every move you and your assistants, **Katie Iannitello** and **Sophie Peoples,** made was like watching a chess game. The phrase "attention to detail" must have been inspired by you!

Bee Berrie, who put my recipes to the test in her own kitchen. A big thank-you for all the thoughtful feedback!

Everyone else on the DK team who played a vital role in hatching this baby: Publisher **Mike Sanders,** I remain humbled and honored that you gave this project the green light. Art director **Bill Thomas** and designers **Jessica Lee** and **Robbie Jones,** I couldn't be more thrilled by how you pulled these many puzzle parts together into one beautiful package. Editorial assistant **Resham Anand,** copyeditor **Mira S. Park,** proofreaders **West Matuszak** and **Bianca Bosman,** and indexer **Beverlee Day**—your sharp eagle eyes were appreciated more than you can imagine!

My incredible team of cheerleaders: **Jenna Noel Salazar, December Brown, Ariana Naim, Maggie Hedera, Jessica Lancaster, Josephina Hellu Sanchez, Sarah Winkler, Ingrida Jasilioniene, Delia St. Pierre, Laurie Jeffries Dugan, Tara Birch, and Aimée Birch.** You never once laughed at my vision, never told me it was impossible, even at my age. You all hopped on the bus and said, "Put the pedal to the metal"—advice worth its weight in gold!

My team at Gersh: **Jade Sherman, Sydney Rosenzweig,** and **Mark Turner.** You all make my life so much easier! Thank you for encouraging authenticity over deals.

The invaluable gals at Shore Fire: **Andrea Evenson, Jaclyn Childress, Lucy Benish,** and **Maria Eilert.** You sure lit a fire under me, and I'm so thankful!

Most of all, I want to thank **YOU.** Whether you've been following me on social media or you're just now getting to know me through the recipes I've shared in this book, I am here for you and because of you, and I will never forget that. I'm thrilled you're on this journey with me, and I'm excited to see where you and I are going next!

About the Author

Lifestyle expert Lora McLaughlin Peterson is the creator of LORAfied, her social media brand with nearly 3 million followers and counting. She loves sharing easy recipes, budget-saving shopping tips, and practical household hacks for helping people simplify and elevate their everyday lives. Born and raised in Kansas, she developed a love for sharing positive and useful information with others during her longtime career as an Emmy Award–winning TV journalist and former network news correspondent in Los Angeles. Since starting her social media platform in 2021, she has demonstrated her hacks on *The Today Show's Hoda & Jenna, Jenna & Friends,* and *LIVE with Kelly and Mark* and has been featured in numerous media outlets, including *The New York Post, Newsweek, Woman's World,* and *The Daily Mail.* A mother of three, she lives in Los Angeles with her husband, kids, and two tiny gremlin dogs.